BLARDY

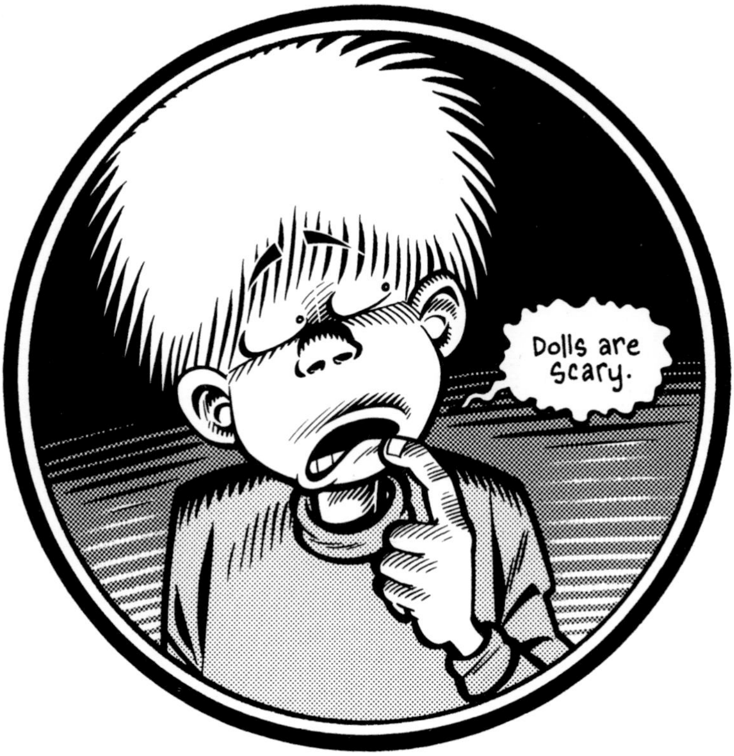
Dolls are scary.

ZOOT SUITE

BEING A COLLECTION OF FINE COMICAL STRIPS
BY THOSE ANTIPODEAN JAPESTERS,
ANDREW AND ROGER LANGRIDGE
(IN CONJUNCTION WITH SEATTLE'S SONS OF FUN, *FANTAGRAPHICS BOOKS*)

WRITTEN BY ANDREW
LANGRIDGE
DRAWN BY ROGER LANGRIDGE
EDITED BY GARY GROTH
PRODUCTION BY DAN DEAN
PUBLISHED BY GARY GROTH
AND KIM THOMPSON

THE AUTHORS WOULD LIKE TO
THANK GARY GROTH, TERI
ROTA, WILLI SAUNDERS,
MELODY MAKER FOR OUR ONLY
REVIEW, AND ANYBODY WE'VE
STOLEN FROM.

PAGES 6 THROUGH 56
ORIGINALLY APPEARED IN
ZOOT! #1-6 (1992-1994); ALL
OTHER MATERIAL APPEARS
HERE FOR THE FIRST TIME.

THE AUTHORS CAN BE
CONTACTED AT THE
FOLLOWING ADDRESS: 132
PARK ROAD, CHISWICK,
LONDON W4 3HP, ENGLAND.

FANTAGRAPHICS BOOKS
7563 LAKE CITY WAY NE
SEATTLE, WA 98115

FIRST EDITION: MARCH, 1998.

ISBN: 1-56097-295-5

TO RECEIVE A FULL-COLOR
CATALOGUE FROM
FANTAGRAPHICS BOOKS, CALL
1-800-657-1100 OR 1-206-
524-1967.

VISIT THE FANTAGRAPHICS
BOOKS WEB SITE AT
WWW.FANTAGRAPHICS.COM

PRINTED IN CANADA.

The JOURNEY HALFWAY

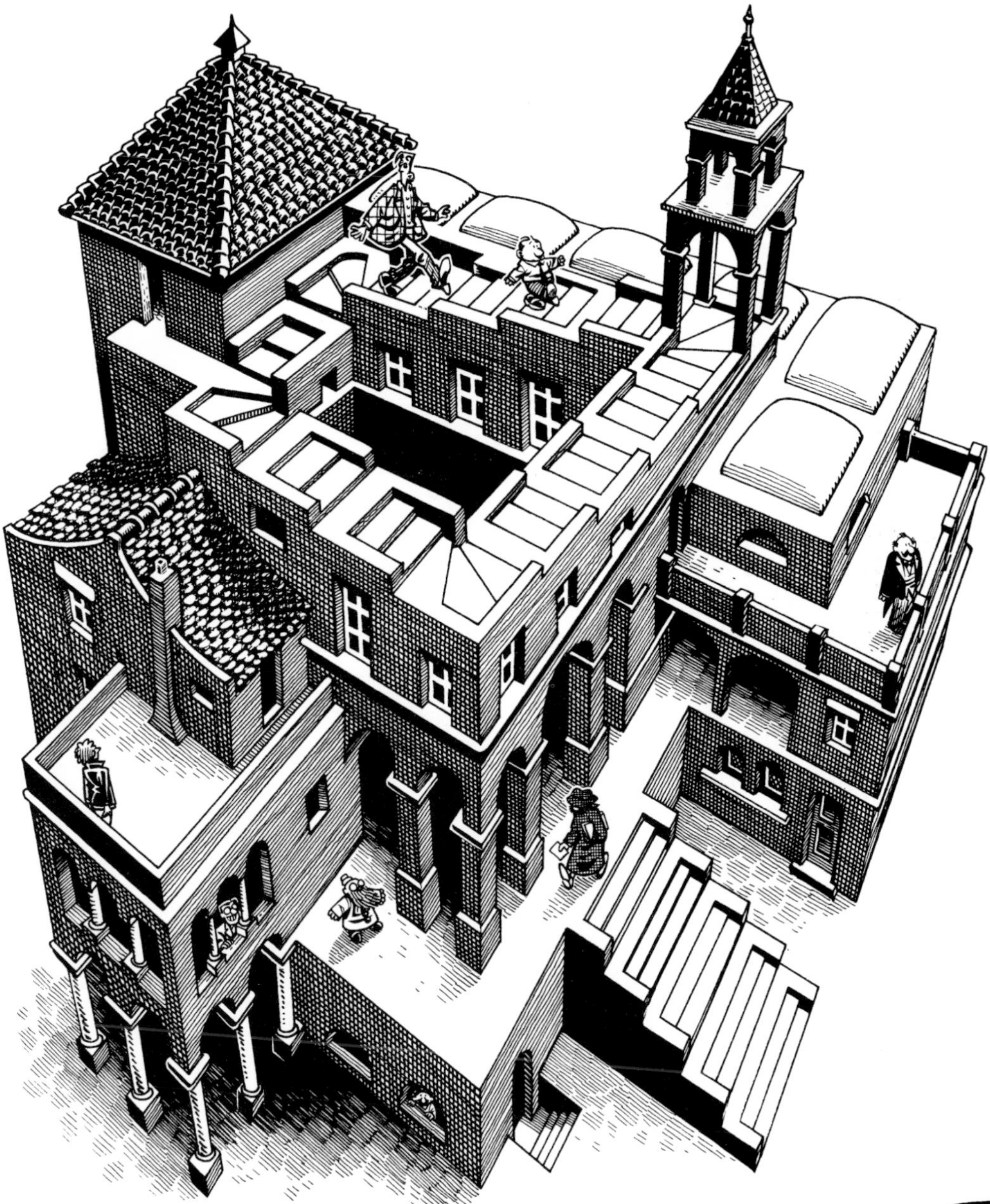

by Andrew and Roger Langridge

The Journey Halfway

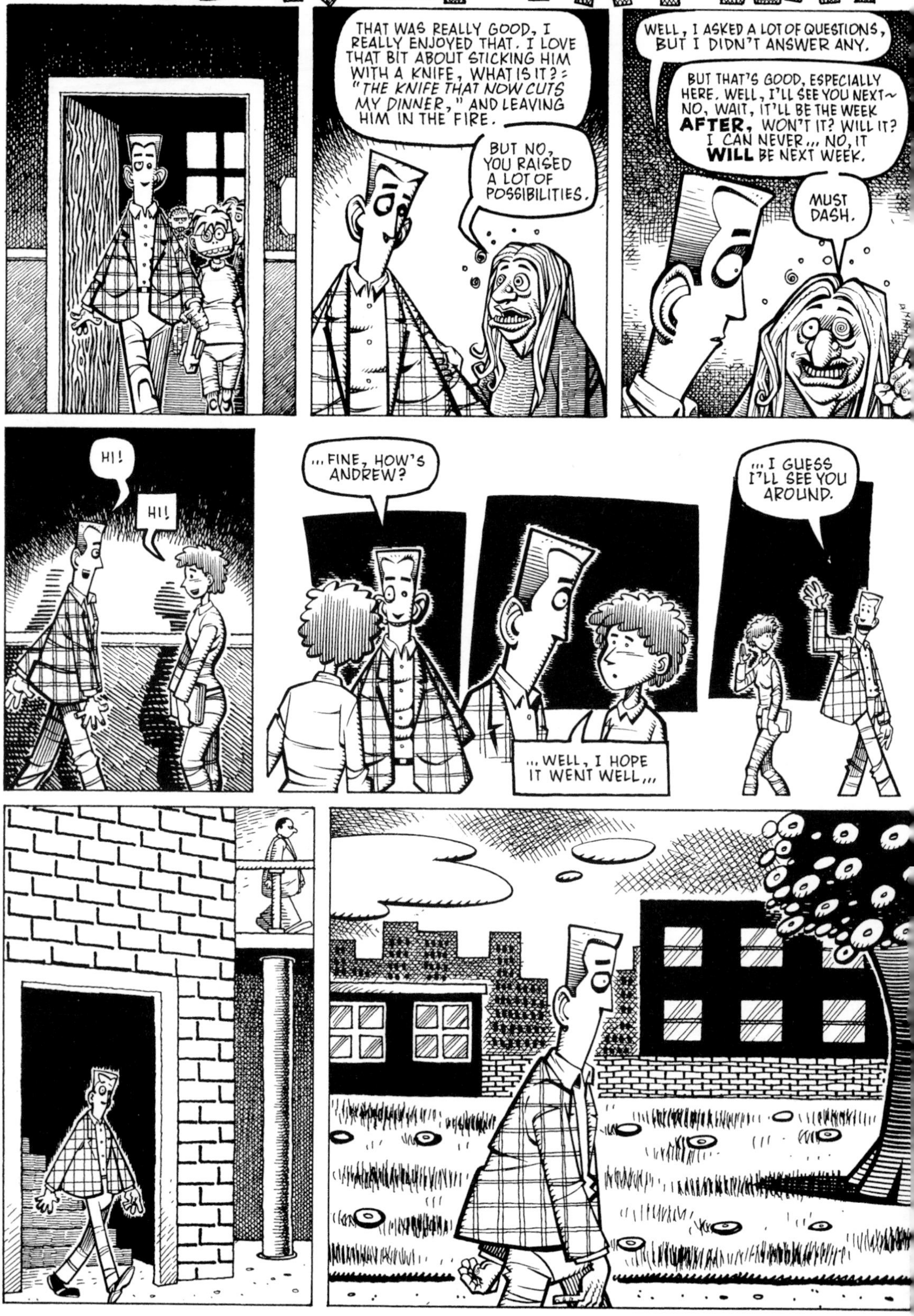
THAT WAS REALLY GOOD, I REALLY ENJOYED THAT. I LOVE THAT BIT ABOUT STICKING HIM WITH A KNIFE, WHAT IS IT? - "THE KNIFE THAT NOW CUTS MY DINNER," AND LEAVING HIM IN THE FIRE.
BUT NO, YOU RAISED A LOT OF POSSIBILITIES.
WELL, I ASKED A LOT OF QUESTIONS, BUT I DIDN'T ANSWER ANY.
BUT THAT'S GOOD, ESPECIALLY HERE. WELL, I'LL SEE YOU NEXT~ NO, WAIT, IT'LL BE THE WEEK AFTER, WON'T IT? WILL IT? I CAN NEVER... NO, IT WILL BE NEXT WEEK.
MUST DASH.
HI!
HI!
...FINE, HOW'S ANDREW?
...WELL, I HOPE IT WENT WELL...
...I GUESS I'LL SEE YOU AROUND.

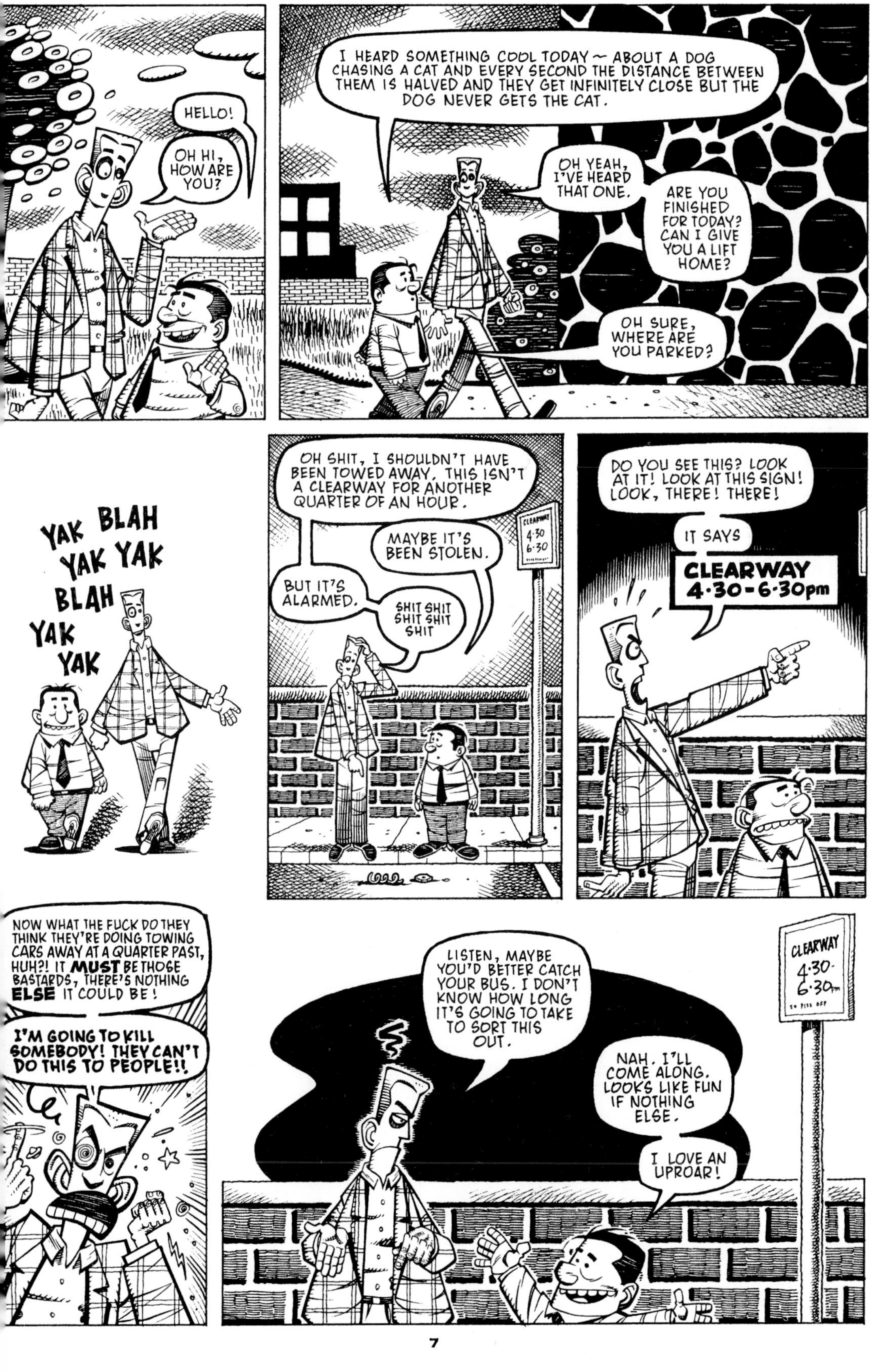
HELLO!
OH HI, HOW ARE YOU?
I HEARD SOMETHING COOL TODAY ~ ABOUT A DOG CHASING A CAT AND EVERY SECOND THE DISTANCE BETWEEN THEM IS HALVED AND THEY GET INFINITELY CLOSE BUT THE DOG NEVER GETS THE CAT.
OH YEAH, I'VE HEARD THAT ONE.
ARE YOU FINISHED FOR TODAY? CAN I GIVE YOU A LIFT HOME?
OH SURE, WHERE ARE YOU PARKED?
YAK BLAH YAK YAK BLAH YAK YAK
OH SHIT, I SHOULDN'T HAVE BEEN TOWED AWAY. THIS ISN'T A CLEARWAY FOR ANOTHER QUARTER OF AN HOUR.
MAYBE IT'S BEEN STOLEN.
BUT IT'S ALARMED.
SHIT SHIT SHIT SHIT SHIT
CLEARWAY 4·30 6·30
DO YOU SEE THIS? LOOK AT IT! LOOK AT THIS SIGN! LOOK, THERE! THERE!
IT SAYS
CLEARWAY 4·30-6·30pm
NOW WHAT THE FUCK DO THEY THINK THEY'RE DOING TOWING CARS AWAY AT A QUARTER PAST, HUH?! IT MUST BE THOSE BASTARDS, THERE'S NOTHING ELSE IT COULD BE!
I'M GOING TO KILL SOMEBODY! THEY CAN'T DO THIS TO PEOPLE!!
LISTEN, MAYBE YOU'D BETTER CATCH YOUR BUS. I DON'T KNOW HOW LONG IT'S GOING TO TAKE TO SORT THIS OUT.
CLEARWAY 4·30-6·30pm
SO PISS OFF
NAH. I'LL COME ALONG. LOOKS LIKE FUN IF NOTHING ELSE.
I LOVE AN UPROAR!

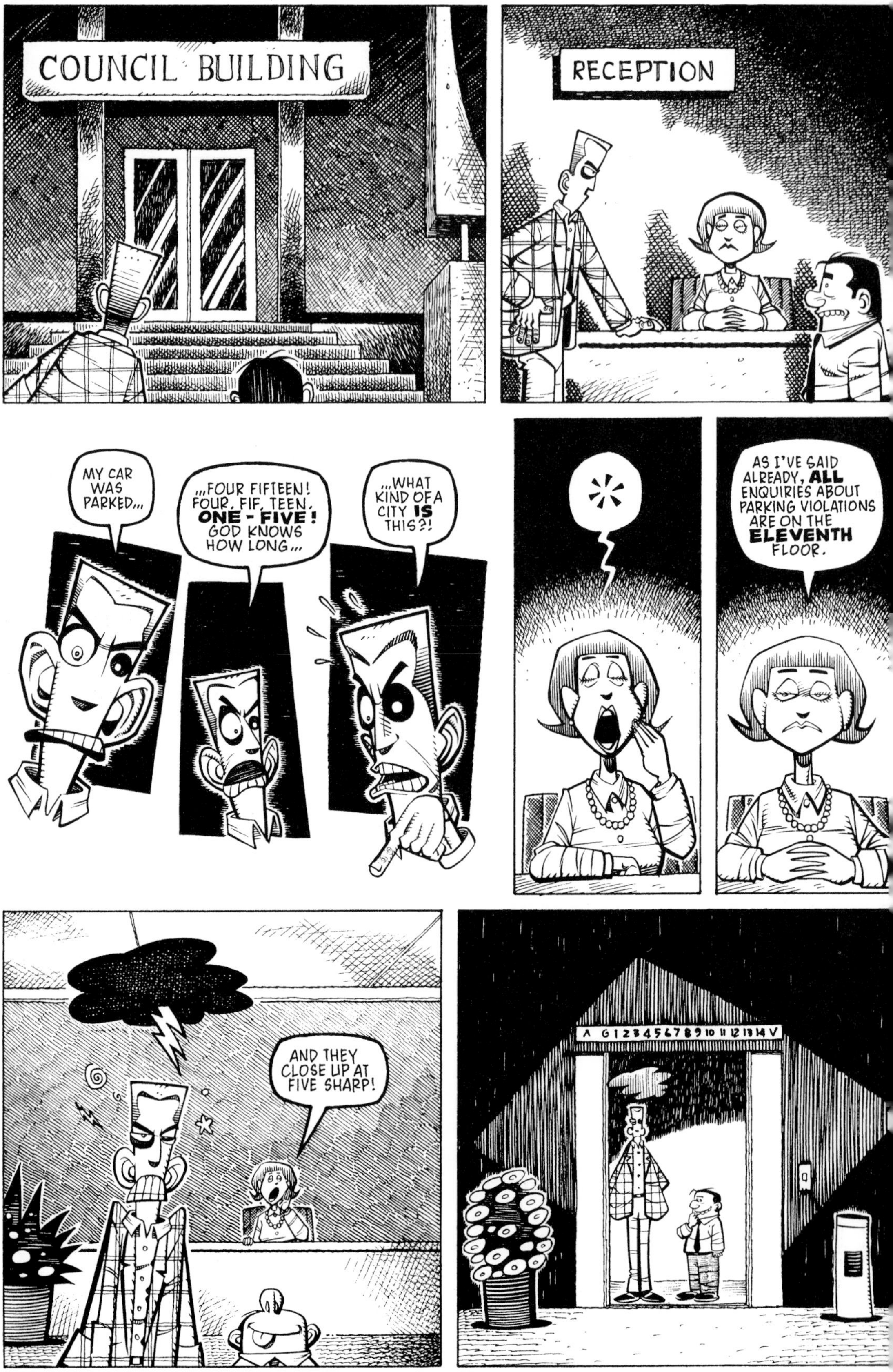
COUNCIL BUILDING
RECEPTION
MY CAR WAS PARKED...
...FOUR FIFTEEN! FOUR. FIF. TEEN. ONE - FIVE! GOD KNOWS HOW LONG...
...WHAT KIND OF A CITY IS THIS?!
AS I'VE SAID ALREADY, ALL ENQUIRIES ABOUT PARKING VIOLATIONS ARE ON THE ELEVENTH FLOOR.
AND THEY CLOSE UP AT FIVE SHARP!
A G 1 2 3 4 5 6 7 8 9 10 11 12 13 14 V

OH, THIS IS NOTHING TO DO WITH US ~ WE HANDLE IMMIGRATION QUERIES. TRY THE TENTH FLOOR ~ ASK FOR **SIMON.**

BAA

OUT OF ORDER

HAVE A NICE WEEKEND!

10

HELLO, CAN I SEE ... IS IT **SIMON,** PLEASE?

MISTER BA~AATES!

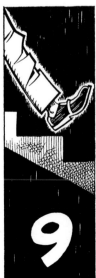

HI, I'M SIMON ~ HOW MAY I HELP YOU?

OH, SORRY. YEAH, THIS **IS** THE LEGAL DEPARTMENT, BUT WE DON'T HANDLE IMPOUNDED VEHICLES. I'D SUGGEST TRAFFIC ON **FIVE** ~ WAIT, IT MIGHT BE SIX.

9

CATERING ↓

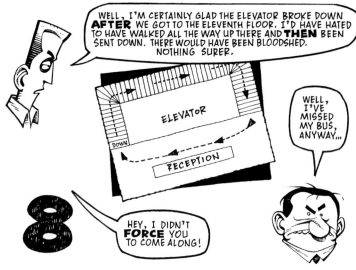

WELL, I'M CERTAINLY GLAD THE ELEVATOR BROKE DOWN **AFTER** WE GOT TO THE ELEVENTH FLOOR. I'D HAVE HATED TO HAVE WALKED ALL THE WAY UP THERE AND **THEN** BEEN SENT DOWN. THERE WOULD HAVE BEEN BLOODSHED, NOTHING SURER.

ELEVATOR

DOWN

RECEPTION

WELL, I'VE MISSED MY BUS, ANYWAY...

8

HEY, I DIDN'T **FORCE** YOU TO COME ALONG!

WHY THE **HELL** COULDN'T THE ARCHITECT HAVE PUT ONE NICE COMPACT STAIRWELL ON **ONE** SIDE OF THE ELEVATOR SHAFT INSTEAD OF THIS PREPOSTEROUS LAZY SPIRAL OF A THING?! IT'S LIKE ONE OF THOSE DEPARTMENT STORES WHERE YOU HAVE TO WALK PAST EVERYTHING TO GET TO WHERE YOU WANT TO GO!

TETCHY, TETCHY

ACCOUNTIN'

7

!

SPLOOSH

WHAT THE HELL'S HAPPENED HERE?!

THE MEN'S TOILET HAS FLOODED ~ AGAIN. I'M JUST FURIOUS, THEY SAID THEY HAD IT FIXED LAST WEEK.

I'LL **NEVER** GET HOME THE WAY THINGS ARE GOING.

WHO ARE YOU LOOKING FOR? YOU KNOW ALL THE DEPARTMENTS CLOSE AT FIVE?

...TEN TO. I HOPE YOU'RE NOT EXPECTING SPECIAL TREATMENT JUST BECAUSE IT'S A LONG WEEKEND.

DON'T GET YOUR WIG IN A TANGLE, WE'RE JUST PASSING THROUGH

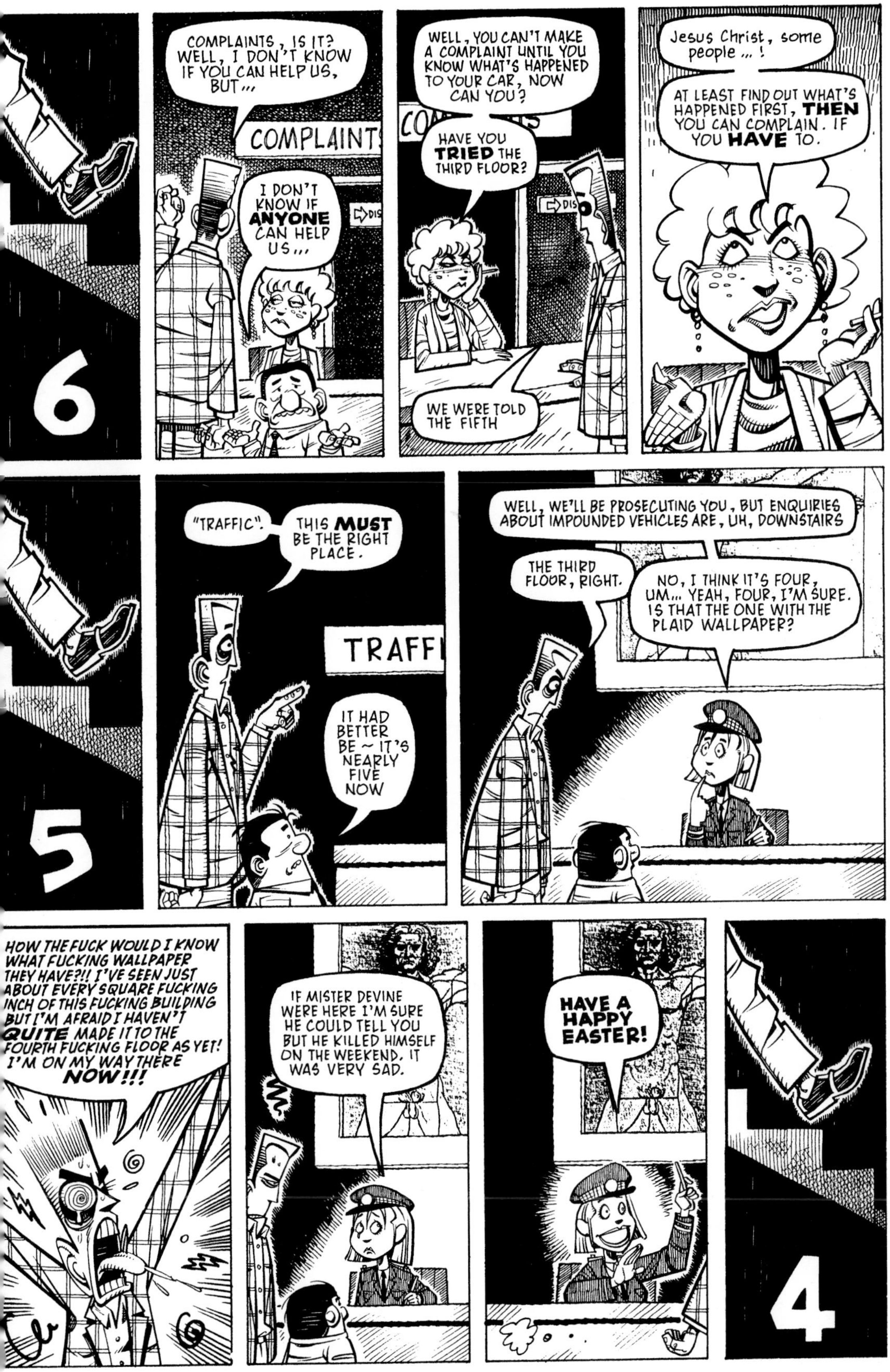
COMPLAINTS, IS IT? WELL, I DON'T KNOW IF YOU CAN HELP US, BUT...
COMPLAINTS
I DON'T KNOW IF ANYONE CAN HELP US...
WELL, YOU CAN'T MAKE A COMPLAINT UNTIL YOU KNOW WHAT'S HAPPENED TO YOUR CAR, NOW CAN YOU?
HAVE YOU TRIED THE THIRD FLOOR?
WE WERE TOLD THE FIFTH
Jesus Christ, some people ... !
AT LEAST FIND OUT WHAT'S HAPPENED FIRST, THEN YOU CAN COMPLAIN. IF YOU HAVE TO.
6
"TRAFFIC".
THIS MUST BE THE RIGHT PLACE.
TRAFFI
IT HAD BETTER BE ~ IT'S NEARLY FIVE NOW
WELL, WE'LL BE PROSECUTING YOU, BUT ENQUIRIES ABOUT IMPOUNDED VEHICLES ARE, UH, DOWNSTAIRS
THE THIRD FLOOR, RIGHT.
NO, I THINK IT'S FOUR, UM... YEAH, FOUR, I'M SURE. IS THAT THE ONE WITH THE PLAID WALLPAPER?
5
HOW THE FUCK WOULD I KNOW WHAT FUCKING WALLPAPER THEY HAVE?!! I'VE SEEN JUST ABOUT EVERY SQUARE FUCKING INCH OF THIS FUCKING BUILDING BUT I'M AFRAID I HAVEN'T QUITE MADE IT TO THE FOURTH FUCKING FLOOR AS YET! I'M ON MY WAY THERE NOW!!!
IF MISTER DEVINE WERE HERE I'M SURE HE COULD TELL YOU BUT HE KILLED HIMSELF ON THE WEEKEND. IT WAS VERY SAD.
HAVE A HAPPY EASTER!
4

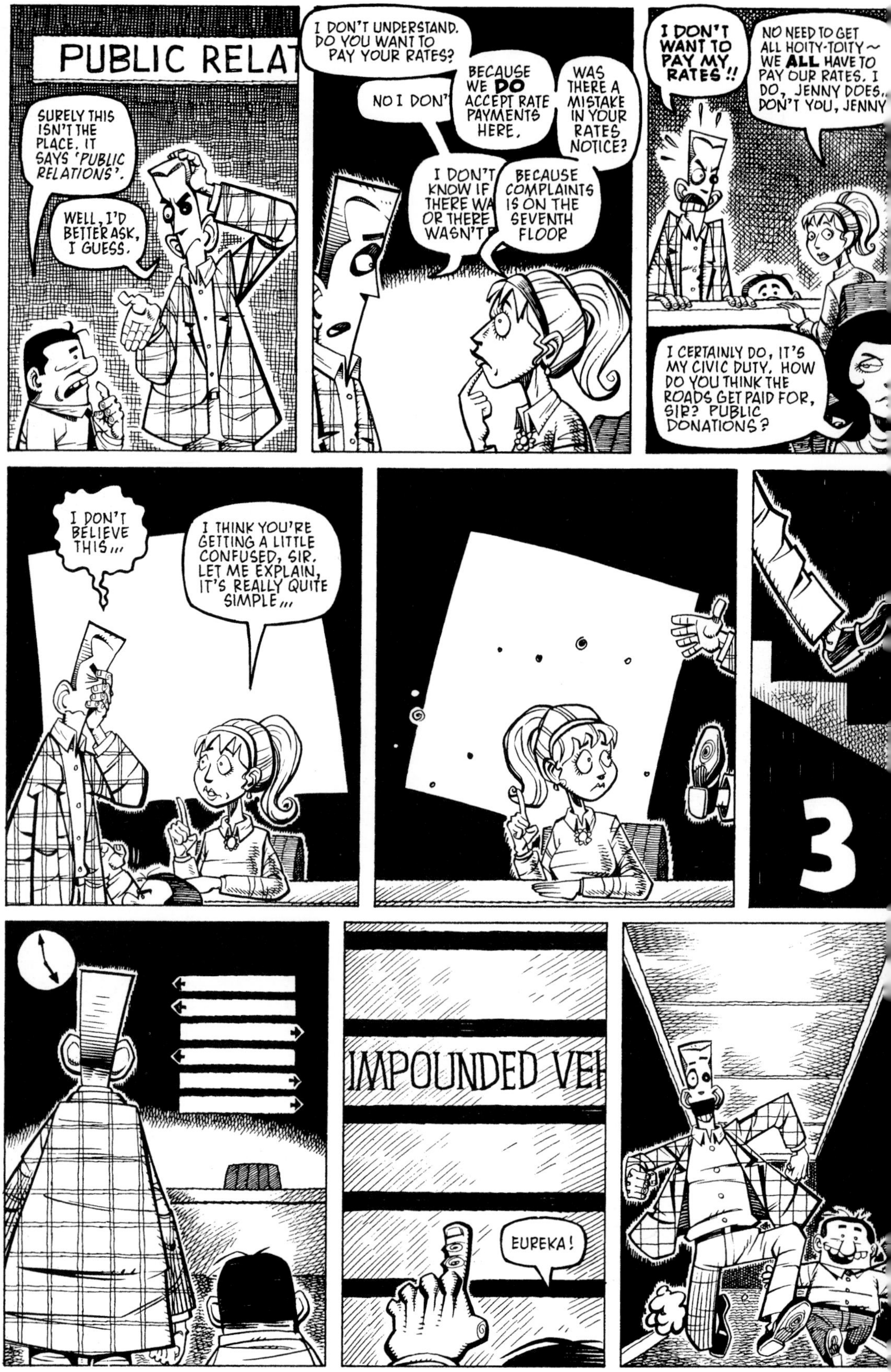
PUBLIC RELAT
SURELY THIS ISN'T THE PLACE. IT SAYS 'PUBLIC RELATIONS'.
WELL, I'D BETTER ASK, I GUESS.
I DON'T UNDERSTAND. DO YOU WANT TO PAY YOUR RATES?
NO I DON'
BECAUSE WE DO ACCEPT RATE PAYMENTS HERE.
WAS THERE A MISTAKE IN YOUR RATES NOTICE?
I DON'T KNOW IF THERE WA OR THERE WASN'T
BECAUSE COMPLAINTS IS ON THE SEVENTH FLOOR
I DON'T WANT TO PAY MY RATES!!
NO NEED TO GET ALL HOITY-TOITY ~ WE ALL HAVE TO PAY OUR RATES. I DO, JENNY DOES.. DON'T YOU, JENNY
I CERTAINLY DO, IT'S MY CIVIC DUTY. HOW DO YOU THINK THE ROADS GET PAID FOR, SIR? PUBLIC DONATIONS?
I DON'T BELIEVE THIS...
I THINK YOU'RE GETTING A LITTLE CONFUSED, SIR. LET ME EXPLAIN. IT'S REALLY QUITE SIMPLE...
3
IMPOUNDED VEH
EUREKA!

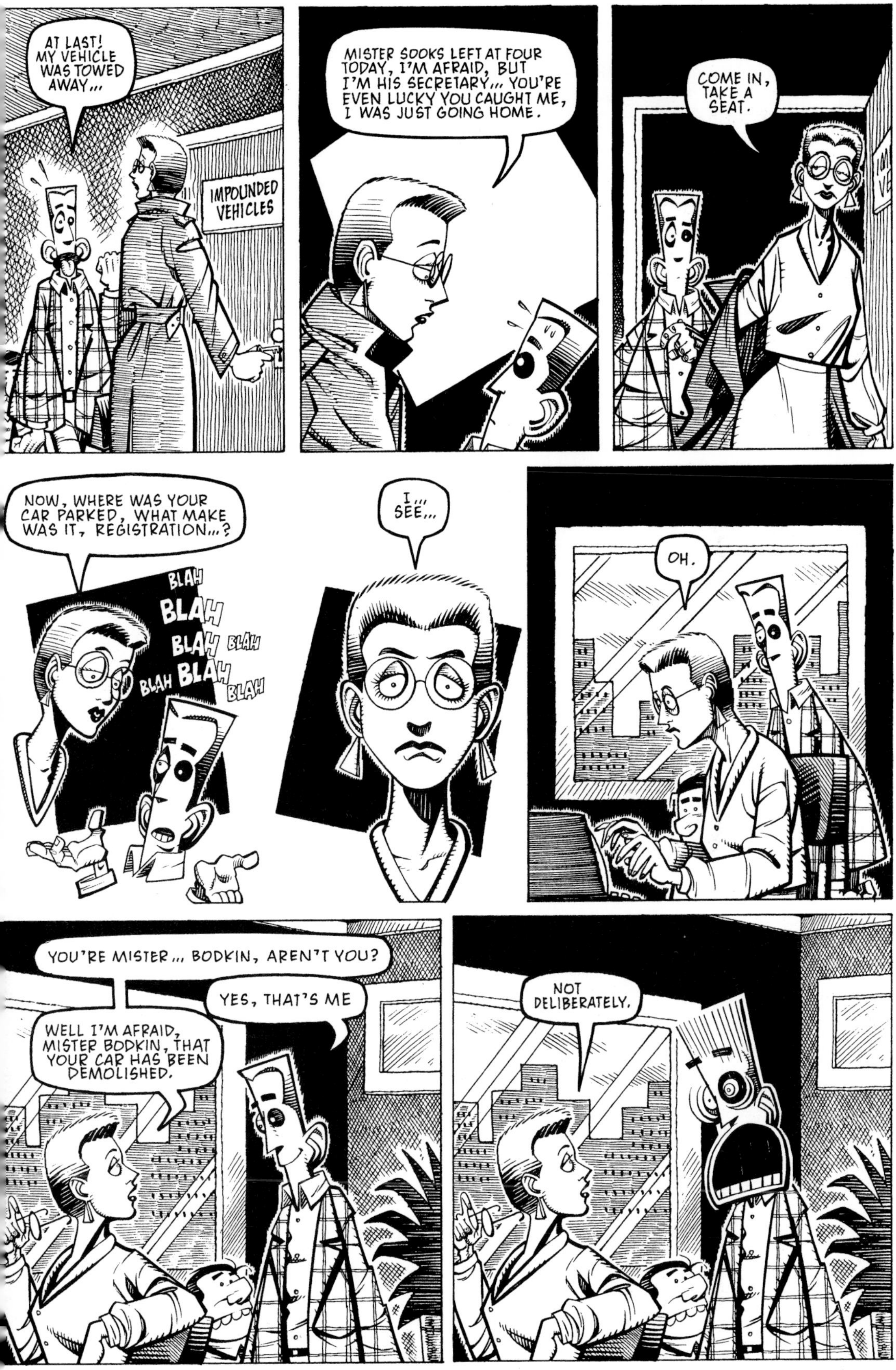
AT LAST! MY VEHICLE WAS TOWED AWAY...
IMPOUNDED VEHICLES
MISTER SOOKS LEFT AT FOUR TODAY, I'M AFRAID, BUT I'M HIS SECRETARY... YOU'RE EVEN LUCKY YOU CAUGHT ME, I WAS JUST GOING HOME.
COME IN, TAKE A SEAT.
NOW, WHERE WAS YOUR CAR PARKED, WHAT MAKE WAS IT, REGISTRATION...?
BLAH BLAH BLAH BLAH BLAH BLAH BLAH
I... SEE...
OH.
YOU'RE MISTER... BODKIN, AREN'T YOU?
YES, THAT'S ME
WELL I'M AFRAID, MISTER BODKIN, THAT YOUR CAR HAS BEEN DEMOLISHED.
NOT DELIBERATELY.

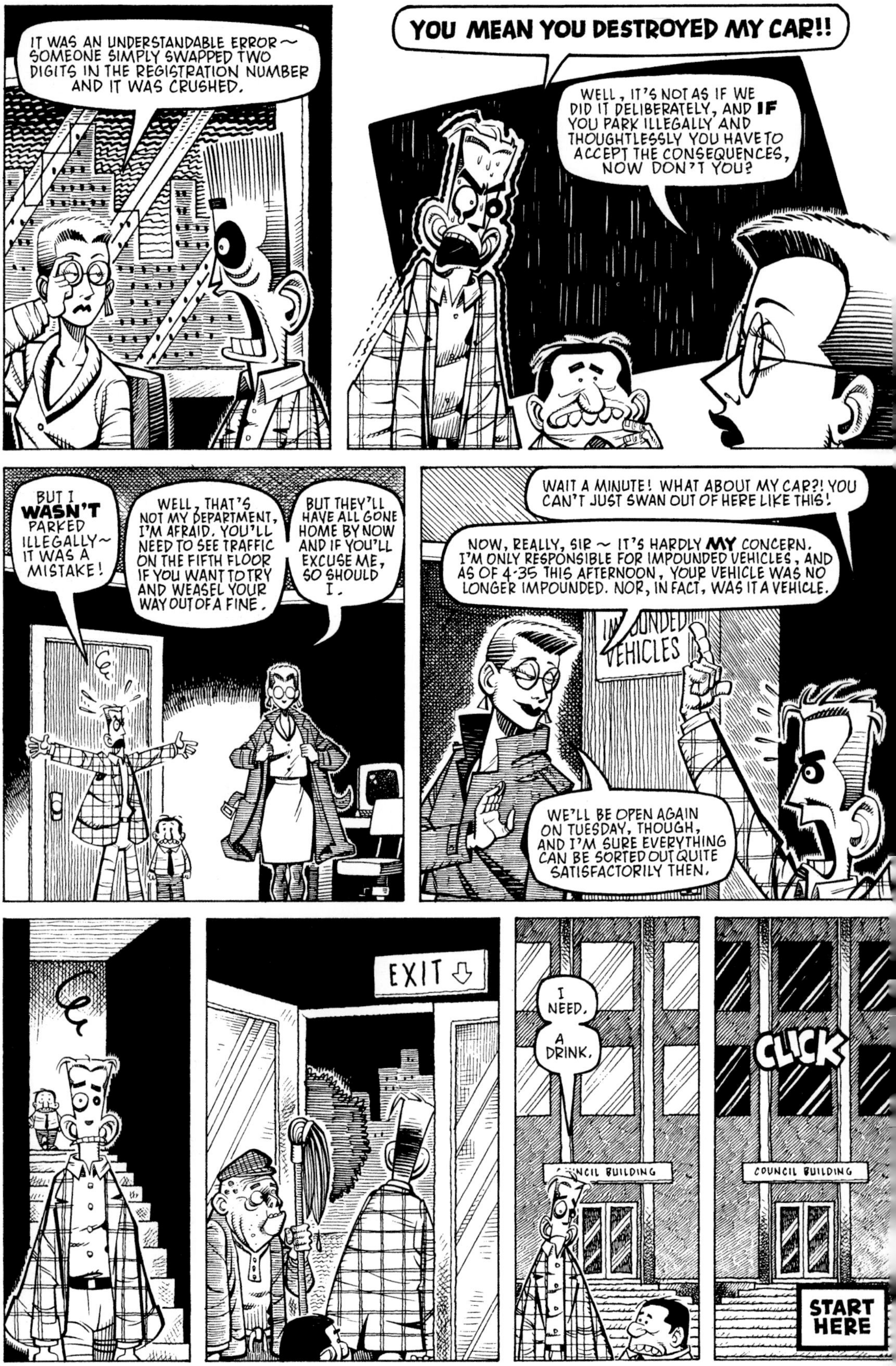
IT WAS AN UNDERSTANDABLE ERROR ~ SOMEONE SIMPLY SWAPPED TWO DIGITS IN THE REGISTRATION NUMBER AND IT WAS CRUSHED.
YOU MEAN YOU DESTROYED MY CAR!!
WELL, IT'S NOT AS IF WE DID IT DELIBERATELY, AND IF YOU PARK ILLEGALLY AND THOUGHTLESSLY YOU HAVE TO ACCEPT THE CONSEQUENCES, NOW DON'T YOU?
BUT I WASN'T PARKED ILLEGALLY ~ IT WAS A MISTAKE!
WELL, THAT'S NOT MY DEPARTMENT, I'M AFRAID. YOU'LL NEED TO SEE TRAFFIC ON THE FIFTH FLOOR IF YOU WANT TO TRY AND WEASEL YOUR WAY OUT OF A FINE.
BUT THEY'LL HAVE ALL GONE HOME BY NOW AND IF YOU'LL EXCUSE ME, SO SHOULD I.
WAIT A MINUTE! WHAT ABOUT MY CAR?! YOU CAN'T JUST SWAN OUT OF HERE LIKE THIS!
NOW, REALLY, SIR ~ IT'S HARDLY MY CONCERN. I'M ONLY RESPONSIBLE FOR IMPOUNDED VEHICLES, AND AS OF 4·35 THIS AFTERNOON, YOUR VEHICLE WAS NO LONGER IMPOUNDED. NOR, IN FACT, WAS IT A VEHICLE.
VEHICLES
WE'LL BE OPEN AGAIN ON TUESDAY, THOUGH, AND I'M SURE EVERYTHING CAN BE SORTED OUT QUITE SATISFACTORILY THEN.
EXIT
I NEED.
A DRINK.
CLICK
COUNCIL BUILDING
START HERE

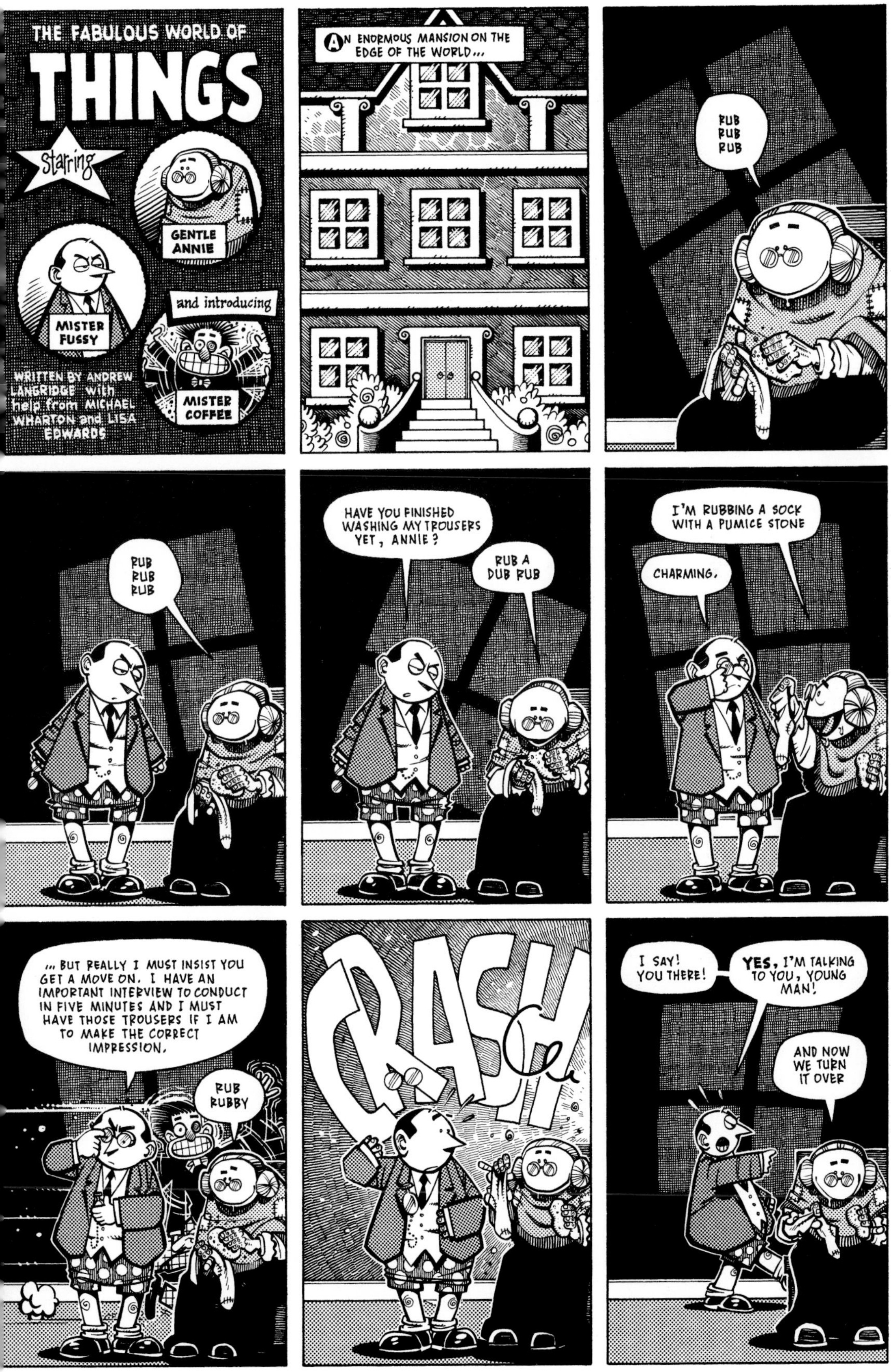
THE FABULOUS WORLD OF
THINGS
starring
GENTLE ANNIE
MISTER FUSSY
and introducing
MISTER COFFEE
WRITTEN BY ANDREW LANGRIDGE with help from MICHAEL WHARTON and LISA EDWARDS
AN ENORMOUS MANSION ON THE EDGE OF THE WORLD...
RUB RUB RUB
RUB RUB RUB
HAVE YOU FINISHED WASHING MY TROUSERS YET, ANNIE?
RUB A DUB RUB
I'M RUBBING A SOCK WITH A PUMICE STONE
CHARMING.
... BUT REALLY I MUST INSIST YOU GET A MOVE ON. I HAVE AN IMPORTANT INTERVIEW TO CONDUCT IN FIVE MINUTES AND I MUST HAVE THOSE TROUSERS IF I AM TO MAKE THE CORRECT IMPRESSION.
RUB RUBBY
CRASH
I SAY! YOU THERE!
YES, I'M TALKING TO YOU, YOUNG MAN!
AND NOW WE TURN IT OVER

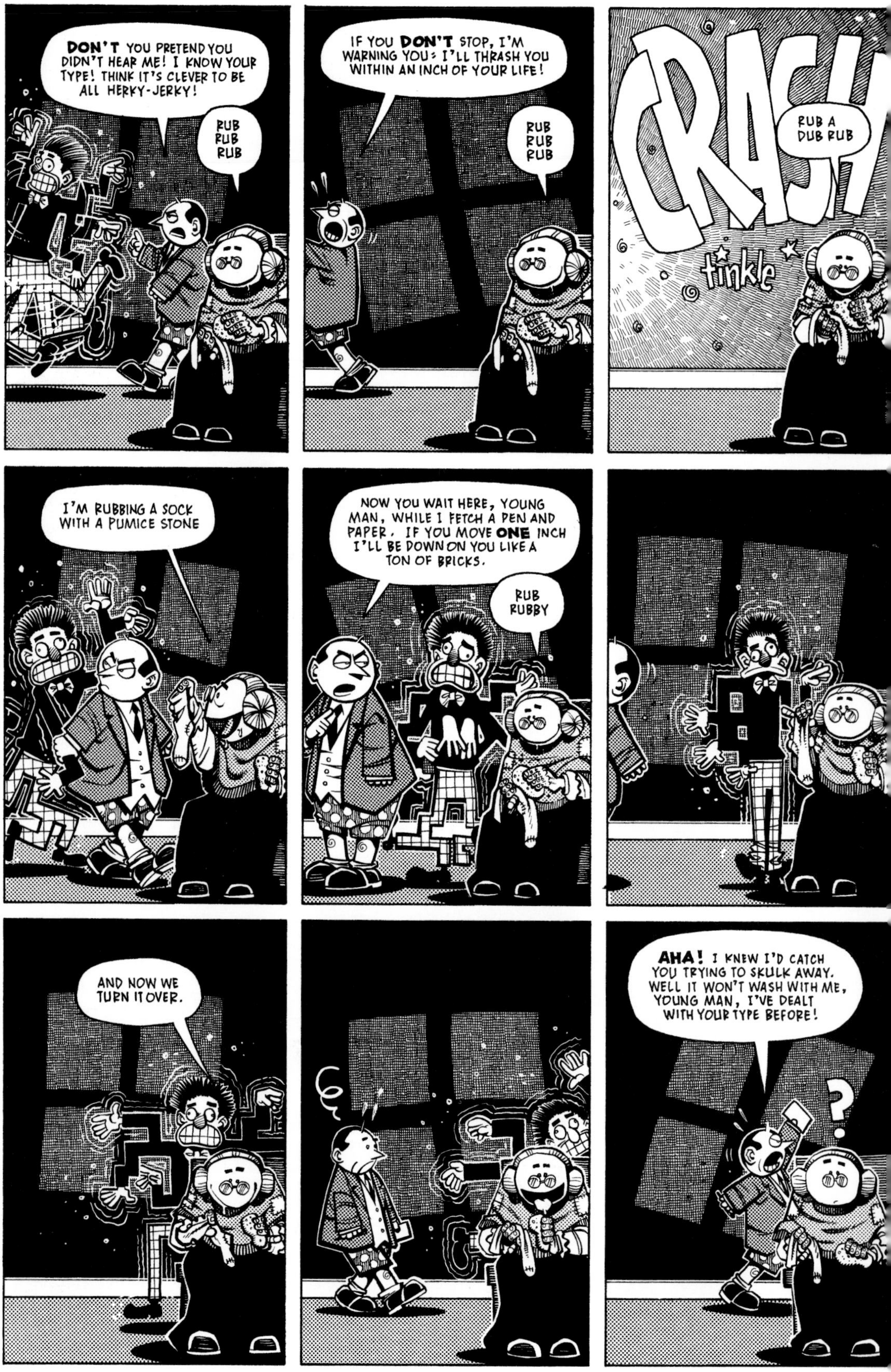
DON'T YOU PRETEND YOU DIDN'T HEAR ME! I KNOW YOUR TYPE! THINK IT'S CLEVER TO BE ALL HERKY-JERKY!
RUB RUB RUB
IF YOU DON'T STOP, I'M WARNING YOU: I'LL THRASH YOU WITHIN AN INCH OF YOUR LIFE!
RUB RUB RUB
CRASH
RUB A DUB RUB
tinkle
I'M RUBBING A SOCK WITH A PUMICE STONE
NOW YOU WAIT HERE, YOUNG MAN, WHILE I FETCH A PEN AND PAPER. IF YOU MOVE ONE INCH I'LL BE DOWN ON YOU LIKE A TON OF BRICKS.
RUB RUBBY
AND NOW WE TURN IT OVER.
AHA! I KNEW I'D CATCH YOU TRYING TO SKULK AWAY. WELL IT WON'T WASH WITH ME, YOUNG MAN, I'VE DEALT WITH YOUR TYPE BEFORE!
?

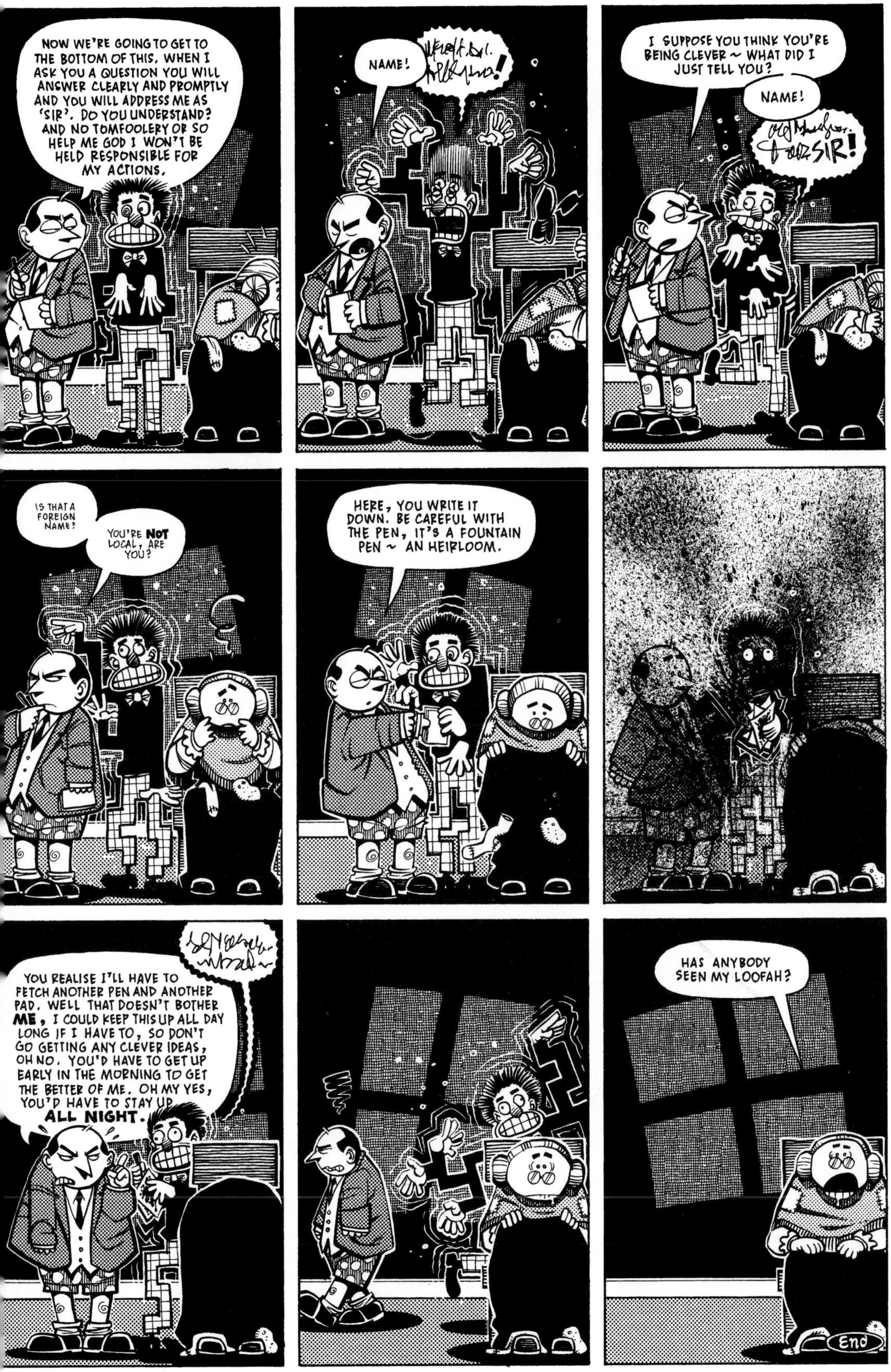
NOW WE'RE GOING TO GET TO THE BOTTOM OF THIS. WHEN I ASK YOU A QUESTION YOU WILL ANSWER CLEARLY AND PROMPTLY AND YOU WILL ADDRESS ME AS 'SIR'. DO YOU UNDERSTAND? AND NO TOMFOOLERY OR SO HELP ME GOD I WON'T BE HELD RESPONSIBLE FOR MY ACTIONS.
NAME!
I SUPPOSE YOU THINK YOU'RE BEING CLEVER ~ WHAT DID I JUST TELL YOU?
NAME!
SIR!
IS THAT A FOREIGN NAME?
YOU'RE NOT LOCAL, ARE YOU?
HERE, YOU WRITE IT DOWN. BE CAREFUL WITH THE PEN, IT'S A FOUNTAIN PEN ~ AN HEIRLOOM.
YOU REALISE I'LL HAVE TO FETCH ANOTHER PEN AND ANOTHER PAD. WELL THAT DOESN'T BOTHER ME, I COULD KEEP THIS UP ALL DAY LONG IF I HAVE TO, SO DON'T GO GETTING ANY CLEVER IDEAS, OH NO. YOU'D HAVE TO GET UP EARLY IN THE MORNING TO GET THE BETTER OF ME. OH MY YES, YOU'D HAVE TO STAY UP ALL NIGHT.
HAS ANYBODY SEEN MY LOOFAH?
End

The JOURNEY HALFWAY

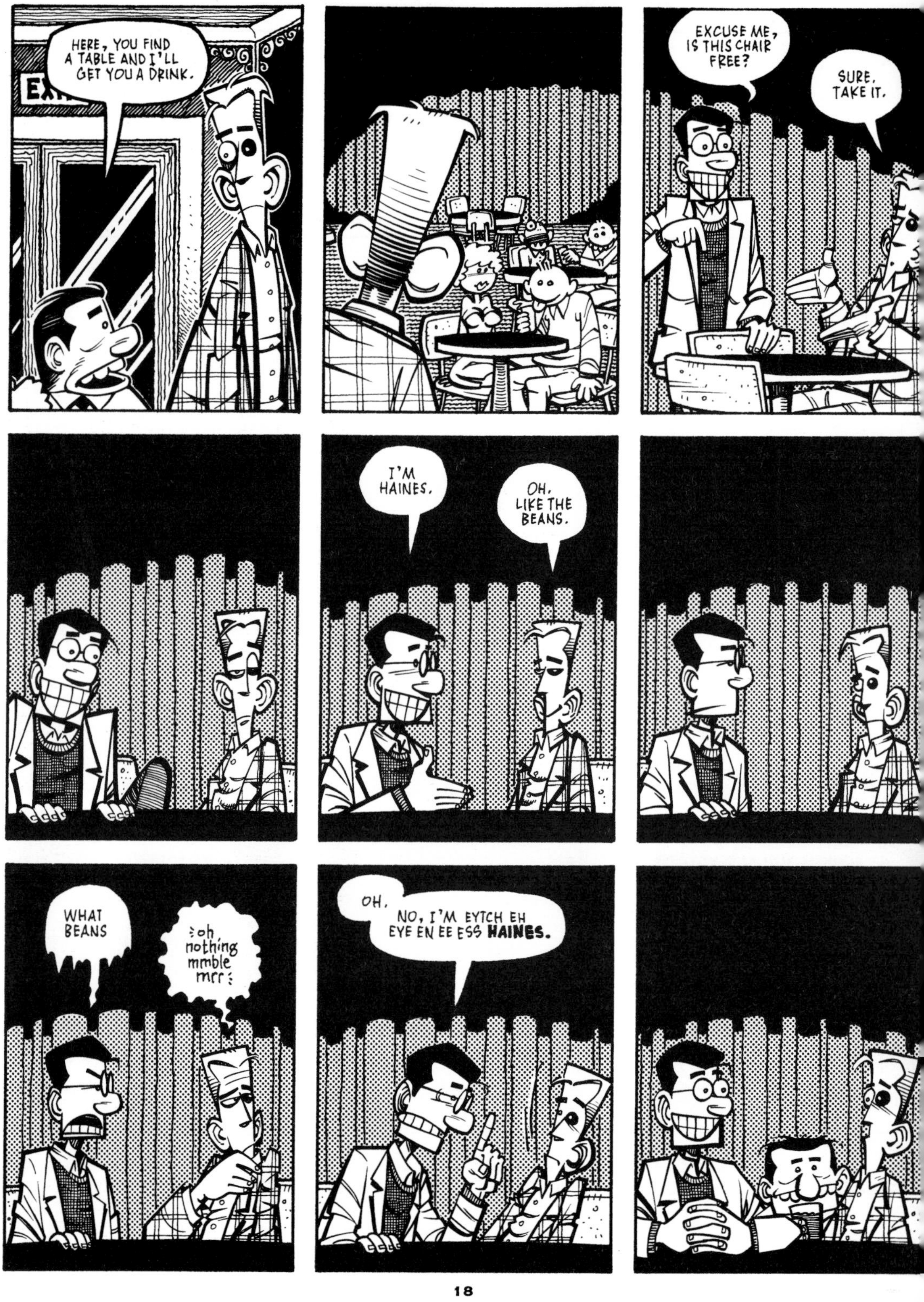

HERE, YOU FIND A TABLE AND I'LL GET YOU A DRINK.
EXCUSE ME, IS THIS CHAIR FREE?
SURE. TAKE IT.
I'M HAINES.
OH. LIKE THE BEANS.
WHAT BEANS
oh nothing mmble mrr
OH.
NO, I'M EYTCH EH EYE EN EE ESS **HAINES.**

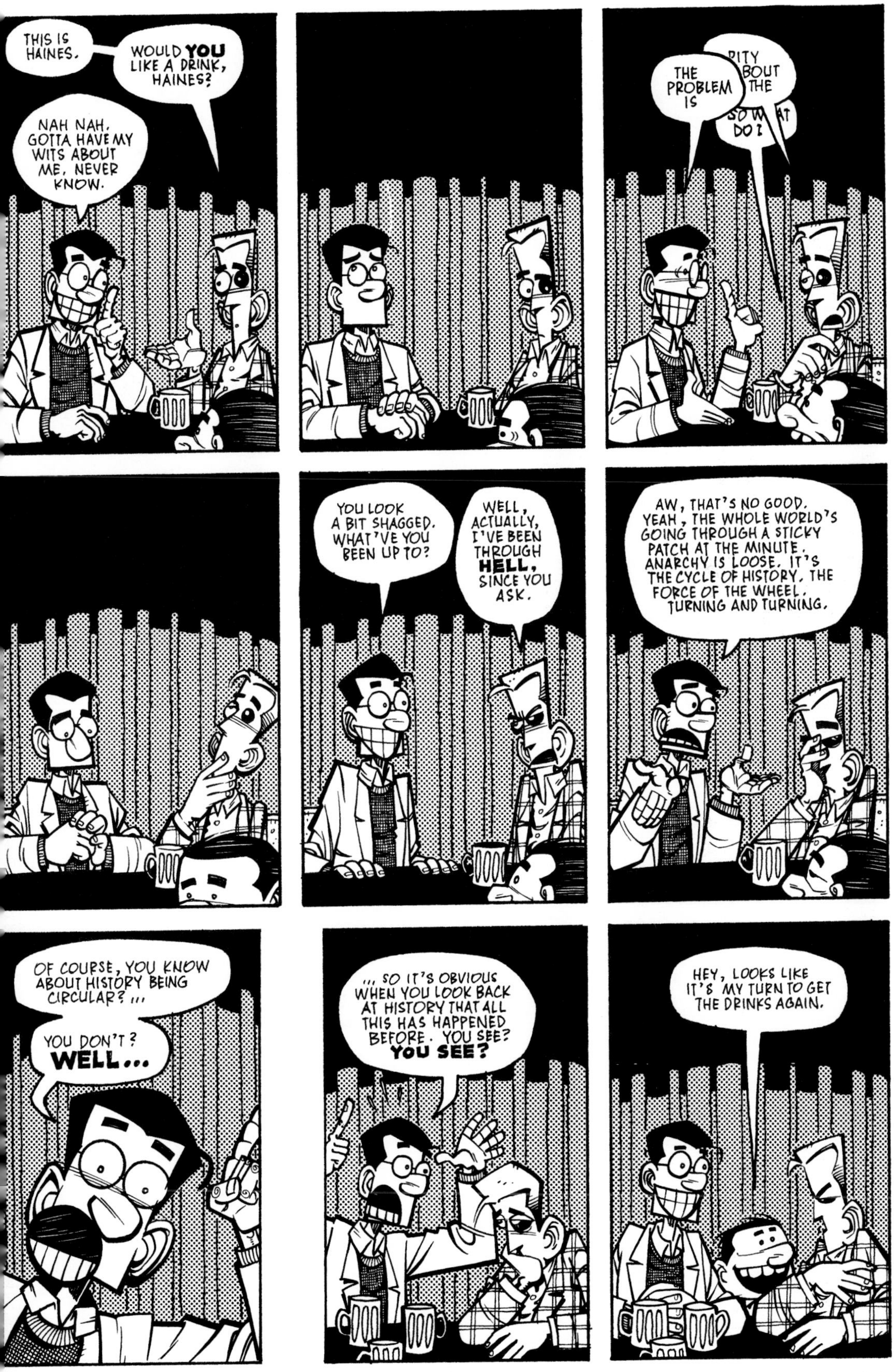
THIS IS HAINES.
WOULD **YOU** LIKE A DRINK, HAINES?
NAH NAH. GOTTA HAVE MY WITS ABOUT ME, NEVER KNOW.
THE PROBLEM IS
YOU LOOK A BIT SHAGGED. WHAT'VE YOU BEEN UP TO?
WELL, ACTUALLY, I'VE BEEN THROUGH **HELL,** SINCE YOU ASK.
AW, THAT'S NO GOOD. YEAH, THE WHOLE WORLD'S GOING THROUGH A STICKY PATCH AT THE MINUTE. ANARCHY IS LOOSE. IT'S THE CYCLE OF HISTORY. THE FORCE OF THE WHEEL. TURNING AND TURNING.
OF COURSE, YOU KNOW ABOUT HISTORY BEING CIRCULAR? ...
YOU DON'T? **WELL...**
... SO IT'S OBVIOUS WHEN YOU LOOK BACK AT HISTORY THAT ALL THIS HAS HAPPENED BEFORE. YOU SEE? **YOU SEE?**
HEY, LOOKS LIKE IT'S MY TURN TO GET THE DRINKS AGAIN.

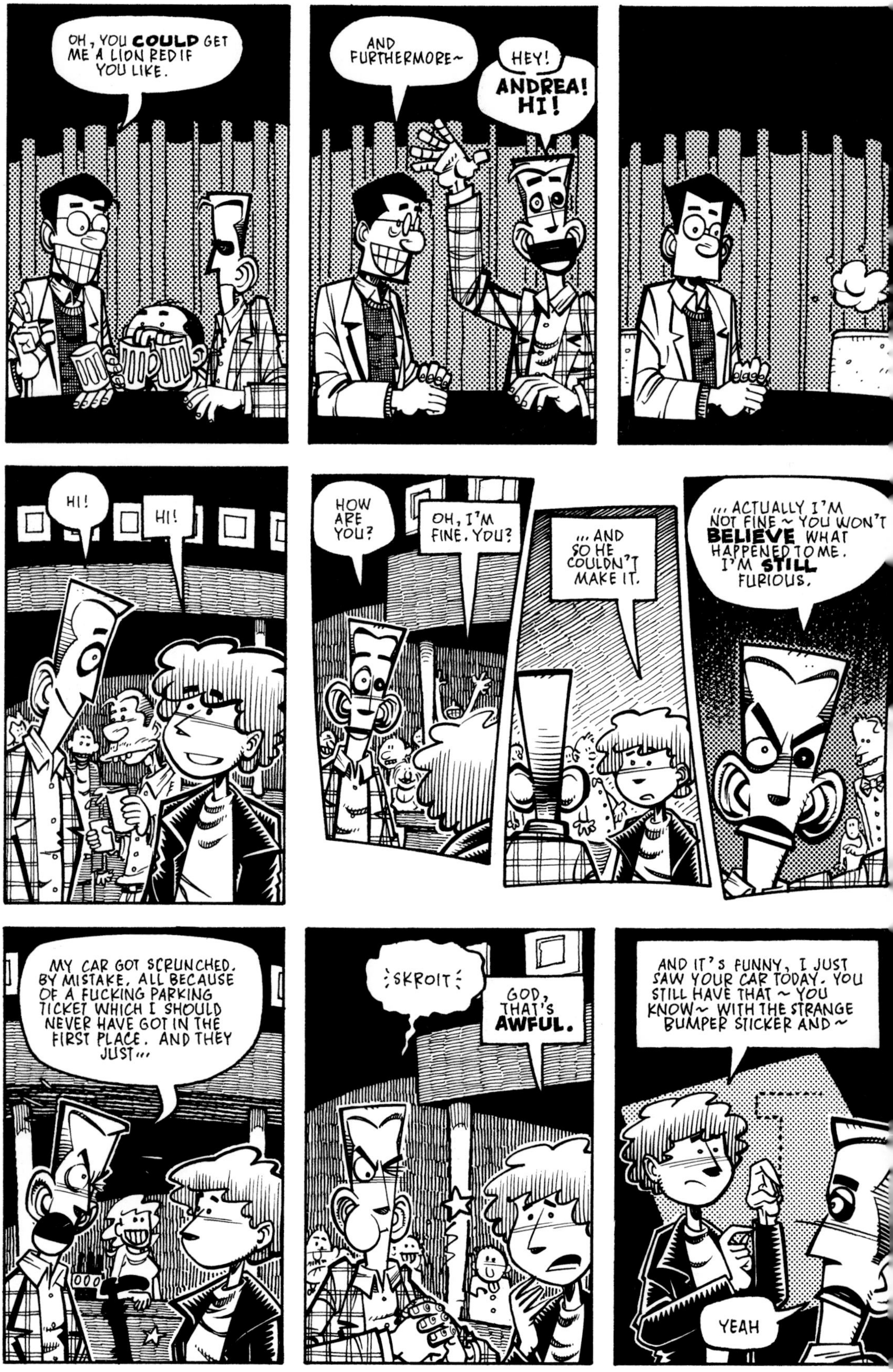
OH, YOU COULD GET ME A LION RED IF YOU LIKE.
AND FURTHERMORE~
HEY! ANDREA! HI!
HI!
HI!
HOW ARE YOU?
OH, I'M FINE. YOU?
... AND SO HE COULDN'T MAKE IT.
... ACTUALLY I'M NOT FINE ~ YOU WON'T BELIEVE WHAT HAPPENED TO ME. I'M STILL FURIOUS.
MY CAR GOT SCRUNCHED. BY MISTAKE. ALL BECAUSE OF A FUCKING PARKING TICKET WHICH I SHOULD NEVER HAVE GOT IN THE FIRST PLACE. AND THEY JUST...
SKROIT
GOD, THAT'S AWFUL.
AND IT'S FUNNY, I JUST SAW YOUR CAR TODAY. YOU STILL HAVE THAT ~ YOU KNOW~ WITH THE STRANGE BUMPER STICKER AND ~
YEAH

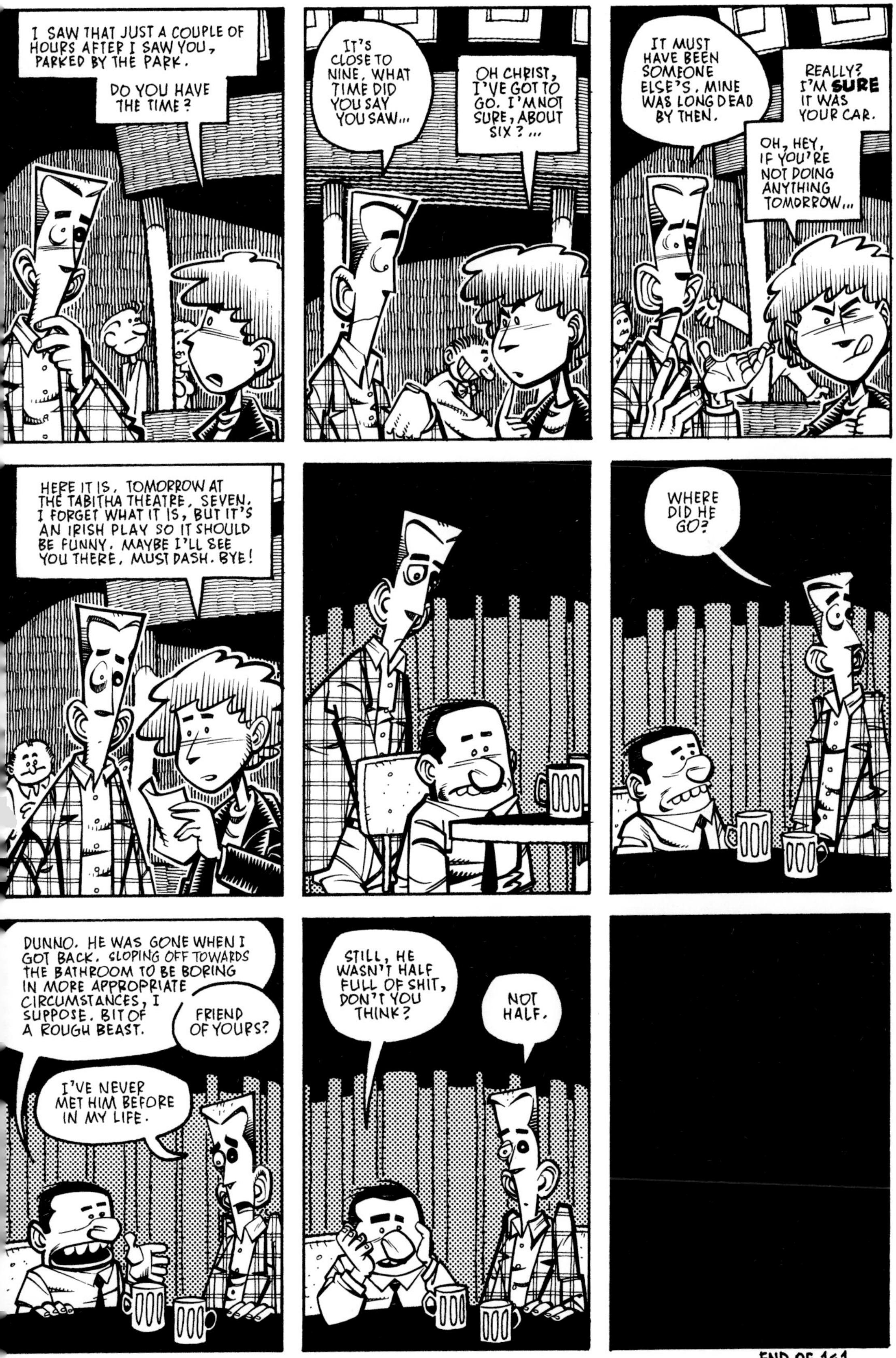
I SAW THAT JUST A COUPLE OF HOURS AFTER I SAW YOU, PARKED BY THE PARK.
DO YOU HAVE THE TIME?
IT'S CLOSE TO NINE. WHAT TIME DID YOU SAY YOU SAW...
OH CHRIST, I'VE GOT TO GO. I'M NOT SURE, ABOUT SIX?...
IT MUST HAVE BEEN SOMEONE ELSE'S. MINE WAS LONG DEAD BY THEN.
REALLY? I'M **SURE** IT WAS YOUR CAR.
OH, HEY, IF YOU'RE NOT DOING ANYTHING TOMORROW...
HERE IT IS, TOMORROW AT THE TABITHA THEATRE, SEVEN. I FORGET WHAT IT IS, BUT IT'S AN IRISH PLAY SO IT SHOULD BE FUNNY. MAYBE I'LL SEE YOU THERE. MUST DASH. BYE!
WHERE DID HE GO?
DUNNO. HE WAS GONE WHEN I GOT BACK. SLOPING OFF TOWARDS THE BATHROOM TO BE BORING IN MORE APPROPRIATE CIRCUMSTANCES, I SUPPOSE. BIT OF A ROUGH BEAST.
FRIEND OF YOURS?
I'VE NEVER MET HIM BEFORE IN MY LIFE.
STILL, HE WASN'T HALF FULL OF SHIT, DON'T YOU THINK?
NOT HALF.

END OF 1=1

The JOURNEY HALFWAY 1:2

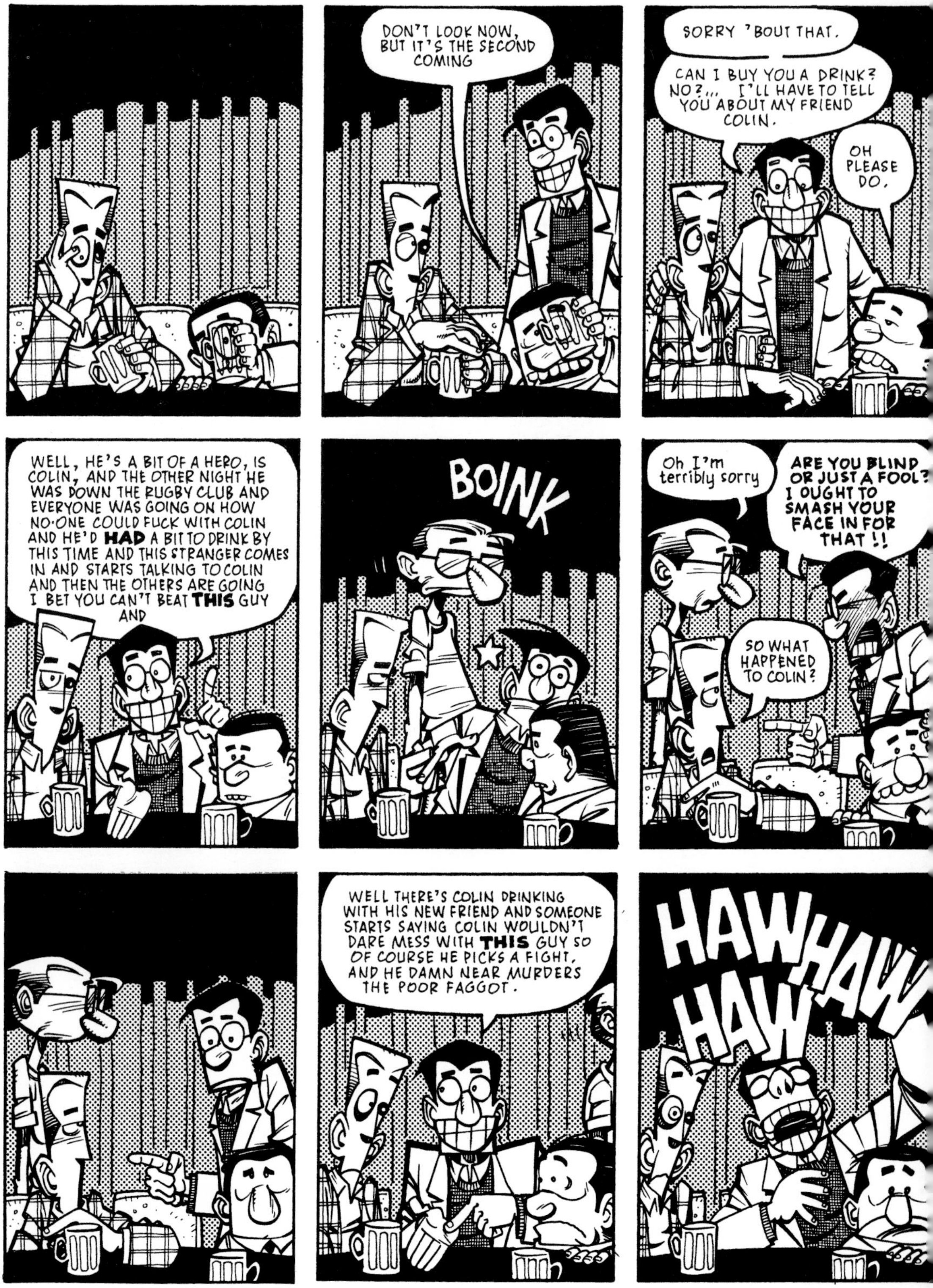

DON'T LOOK NOW, BUT IT'S THE SECOND COMING
SORRY 'BOUT THAT.
CAN I BUY YOU A DRINK? NO?... I'LL HAVE TO TELL YOU ABOUT MY FRIEND COLIN.
OH PLEASE DO.
WELL, HE'S A BIT OF A HERO, IS COLIN, AND THE OTHER NIGHT HE WAS DOWN THE RUGBY CLUB AND EVERYONE WAS GOING ON HOW NO-ONE COULD FUCK WITH COLIN AND HE'D HAD A BIT TO DRINK BY THIS TIME AND THIS STRANGER COMES IN AND STARTS TALKING TO COLIN AND THEN THE OTHERS ARE GOING I BET YOU CAN'T BEAT THIS GUY AND
BOINK
Oh I'm terribly sorry
ARE YOU BLIND OR JUST A FOOL? I OUGHT TO SMASH YOUR FACE IN FOR THAT!!
SO WHAT HAPPENED TO COLIN?
WELL THERE'S COLIN DRINKING WITH HIS NEW FRIEND AND SOMEONE STARTS SAYING COLIN WOULDN'T DARE MESS WITH THIS GUY SO OF COURSE HE PICKS A FIGHT, AND HE DAMN NEAR MURDERS THE POOR FAGGOT.
HAW HAW HAW

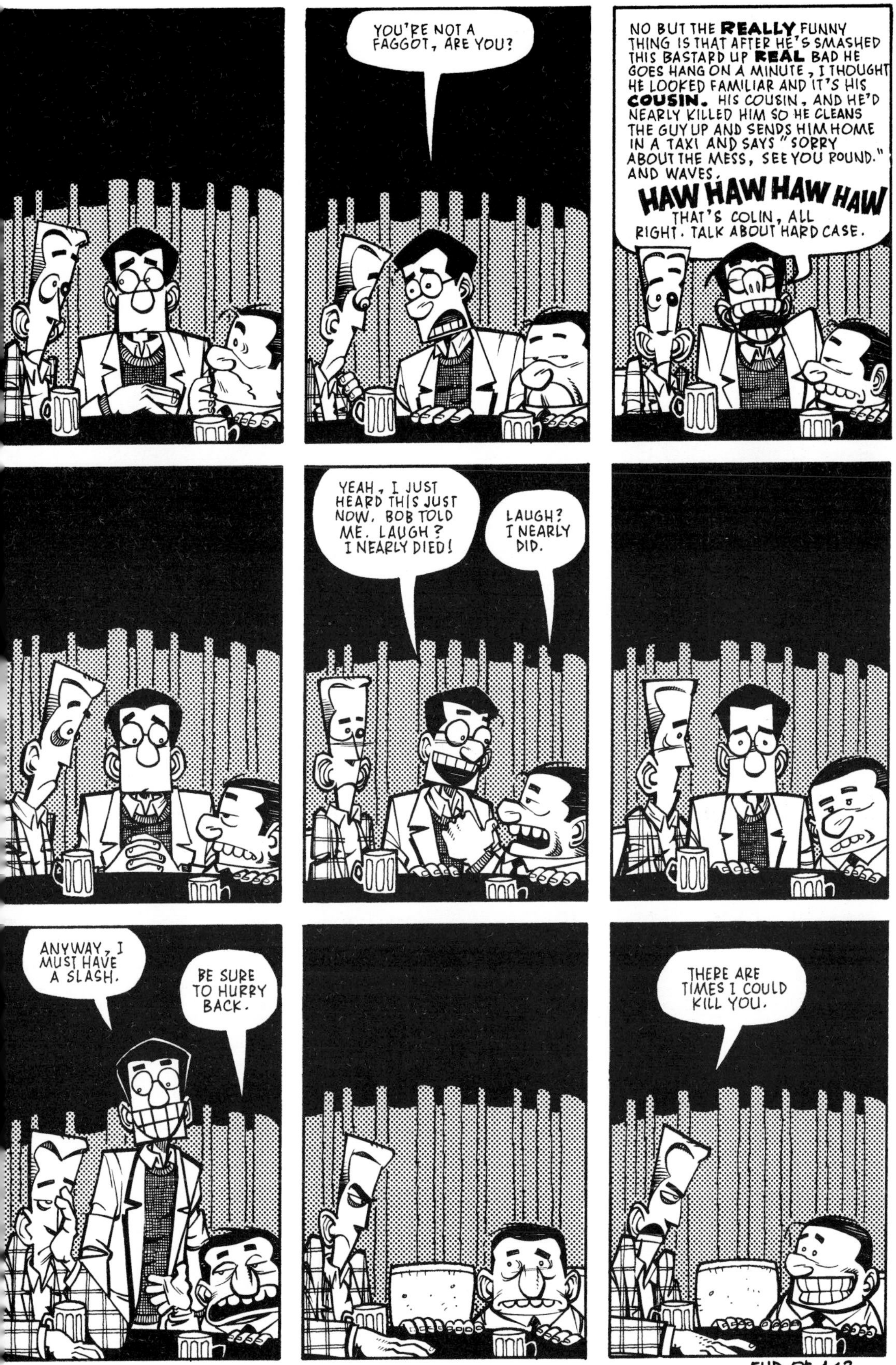
YOU'RE NOT A FAGGOT, ARE YOU?
NO BUT THE REALLY FUNNY THING IS THAT AFTER HE'S SMASHED THIS BASTARD UP REAL BAD HE GOES HANG ON A MINUTE, I THOUGHT HE LOOKED FAMILIAR AND IT'S HIS COUSIN. HIS COUSIN, AND HE'D NEARLY KILLED HIM SO HE CLEANS THE GUY UP AND SENDS HIM HOME IN A TAXI AND SAYS "SORRY ABOUT THE MESS, SEE YOU ROUND." AND WAVES.
HAW HAW HAW HAW
THAT'S COLIN, ALL RIGHT. TALK ABOUT HARD CASE.
YEAH, I JUST HEARD THIS JUST NOW. BOB TOLD ME. LAUGH? I NEARLY DIED!
LAUGH? I NEARLY DID.
ANYWAY, I MUST HAVE A SLASH.
BE SURE TO HURRY BACK.
THERE ARE TIMES I COULD KILL YOU.

END OF 1÷2

The JOURNEY HALFWAY 13

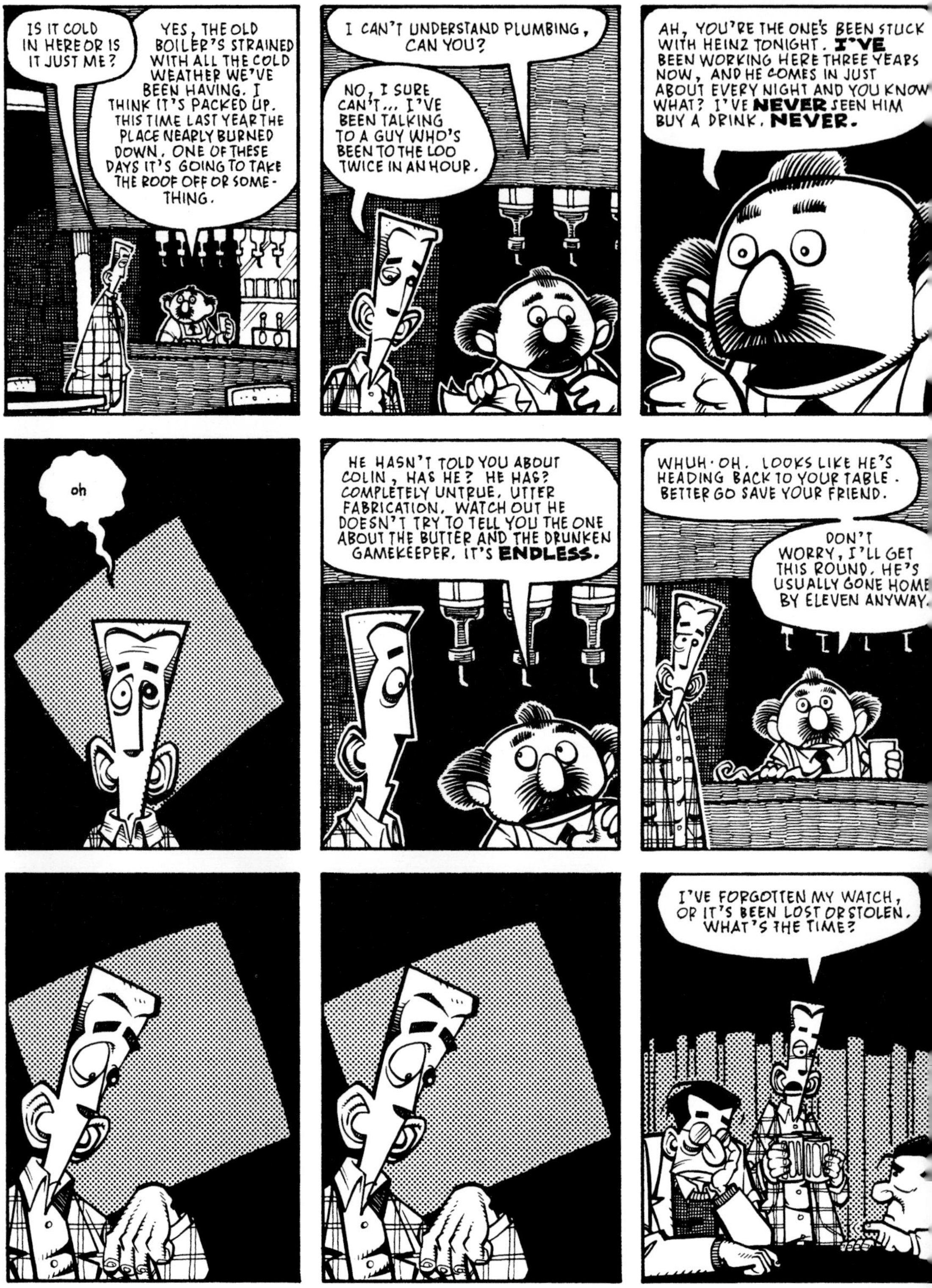
IS IT COLD IN HERE OR IS IT JUST ME?
YES, THE OLD BOILER'S STRAINED WITH ALL THE COLD WEATHER WE'VE BEEN HAVING. I THINK IT'S PACKED UP. THIS TIME LAST YEAR THE PLACE NEARLY BURNED DOWN. ONE OF THESE DAYS IT'S GOING TO TAKE THE ROOF OFF OR SOMETHING.
I CAN'T UNDERSTAND PLUMBING, CAN YOU?
NO, I SURE CAN'T... I'VE BEEN TALKING TO A GUY WHO'S BEEN TO THE LOO TWICE IN AN HOUR.
AH, YOU'RE THE ONE'S BEEN STUCK WITH HEINZ TONIGHT. I'VE BEEN WORKING HERE THREE YEARS NOW, AND HE COMES IN JUST ABOUT EVERY NIGHT AND YOU KNOW WHAT? I'VE NEVER SEEN HIM BUY A DRINK. NEVER.
oh
HE HASN'T TOLD YOU ABOUT COLIN, HAS HE? HE HAS? COMPLETELY UNTRUE. UTTER FABRICATION. WATCH OUT HE DOESN'T TRY TO TELL YOU THE ONE ABOUT THE BUTTER AND THE DRUNKEN GAMEKEEPER. IT'S ENDLESS.
WHUH-OH. LOOKS LIKE HE'S HEADING BACK TO YOUR TABLE. BETTER GO SAVE YOUR FRIEND.
DON'T WORRY, I'LL GET THIS ROUND. HE'S USUALLY GONE HOME BY ELEVEN ANYWAY.
I'VE FORGOTTEN MY WATCH, OR IT'S BEEN LOST OR STOLEN. WHAT'S THE TIME?

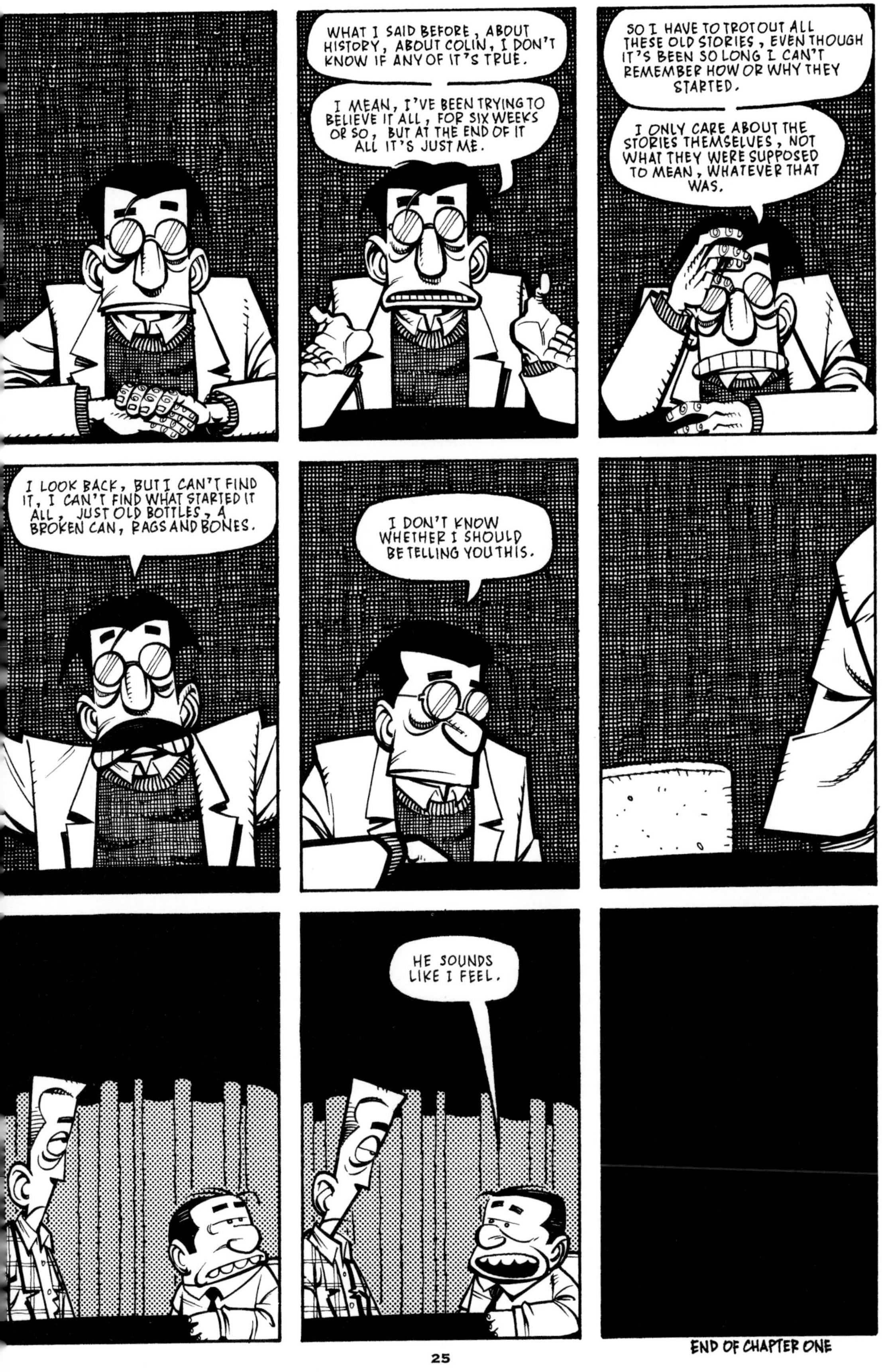
WHAT I SAID BEFORE, ABOUT HISTORY, ABOUT COLIN, I DON'T KNOW IF ANY OF IT'S TRUE.
I MEAN, I'VE BEEN TRYING TO BELIEVE IT ALL, FOR SIX WEEKS OR SO, BUT AT THE END OF IT ALL IT'S JUST ME.
SO I HAVE TO TROT OUT ALL THESE OLD STORIES, EVEN THOUGH IT'S BEEN SO LONG I CAN'T REMEMBER HOW OR WHY THEY STARTED.
I ONLY CARE ABOUT THE STORIES THEMSELVES, NOT WHAT THEY WERE SUPPOSED TO MEAN, WHATEVER THAT WAS.
I LOOK BACK, BUT I CAN'T FIND IT, I CAN'T FIND WHAT STARTED IT ALL, JUST OLD BOTTLES, A BROKEN CAN, RAGS AND BONES.
I DON'T KNOW WHETHER I SHOULD BE TELLING YOU THIS.
HE SOUNDS LIKE I FEEL.

END OF CHAPTER ONE

A Dictionary of Oubliettes

Missuses and Misters. I thank you for your attention and your patience. Today we examine the very interesting subject of French social customs, especially the oubliette.

OUBLIETTE

This family are the words for meetings frustrated and missed. The most well-known but not the most common of these is the 'oubliette'.

'Une oubliette' is an unimportant un·meeting. If you agree to meet your friend and forget to meet your friend, but it is of no importance, this is an oubliette. For example, he forgot to meet also or was killed by a train.

UNE OUBLIETTE

On the other-hand, 'le grand oublier' is the meeting that only one person forgets and the other becomes angry.

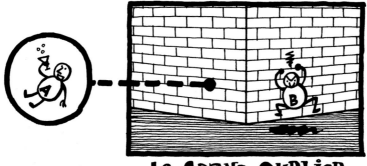

LE GRAND OUBLIER

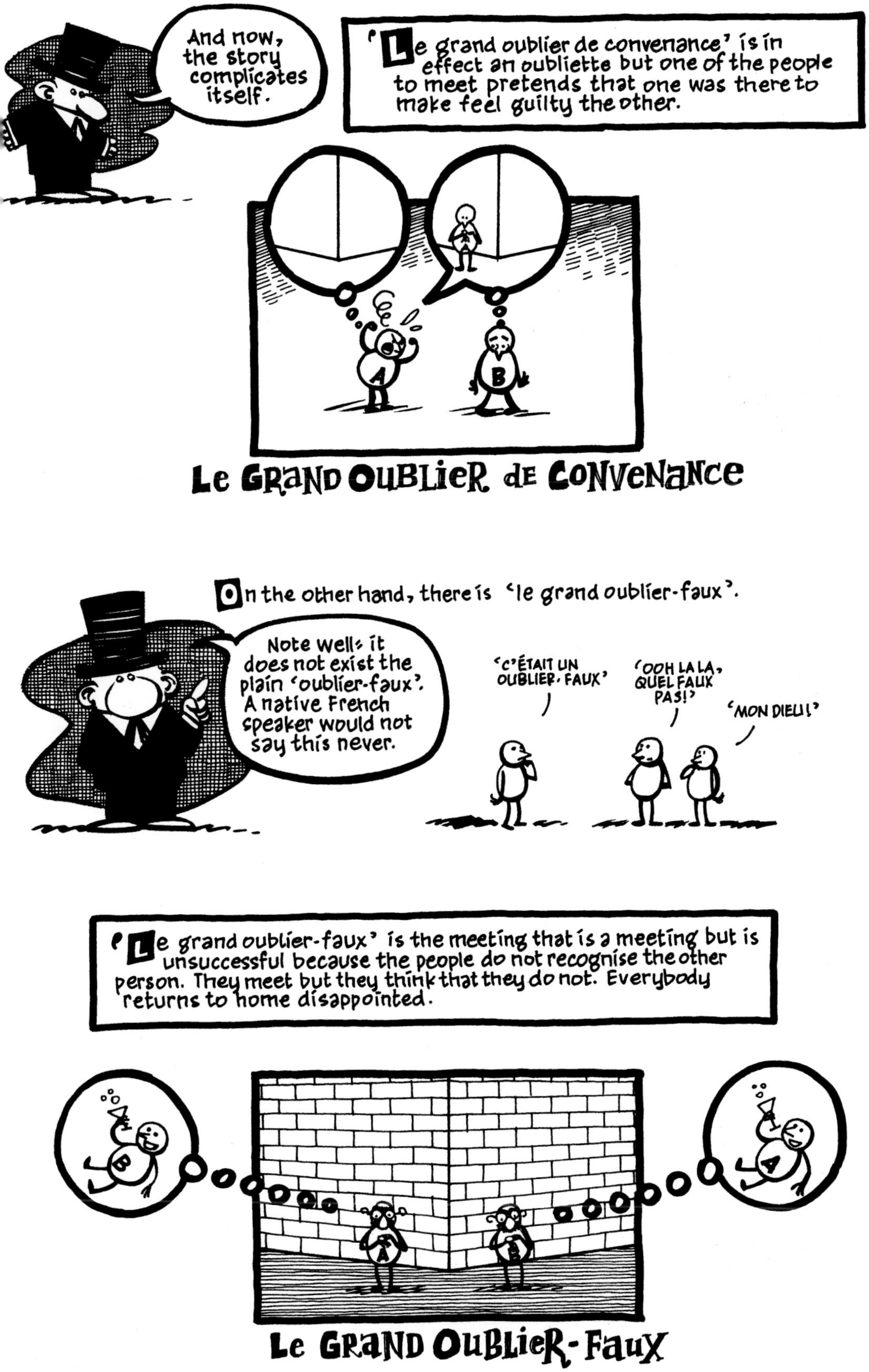
And now, the story complicates itself.
'Le grand oublier de convenance' is in effect an oubliette but one of the people to meet pretends that one was there to make feel guilty the other.
Le Grand Oublier de Convenance
On the other hand, there is 'le grand oublier-faux'.
Note well: it does not exist the plain 'oublier-faux'. A native French speaker would not say this never.
'C'ÉTAIT UN OUBLIER-FAUX'
'OOH LA LA, QUEL FAUX PAS!'
'MON DIEU!'
'Le grand oublier-faux' is the meeting that is a meeting but is unsuccessful because the people do not recognise the other person. They meet but they think that they do not. Everybody returns to home disappointed.
Le Grand Oublier-Faux

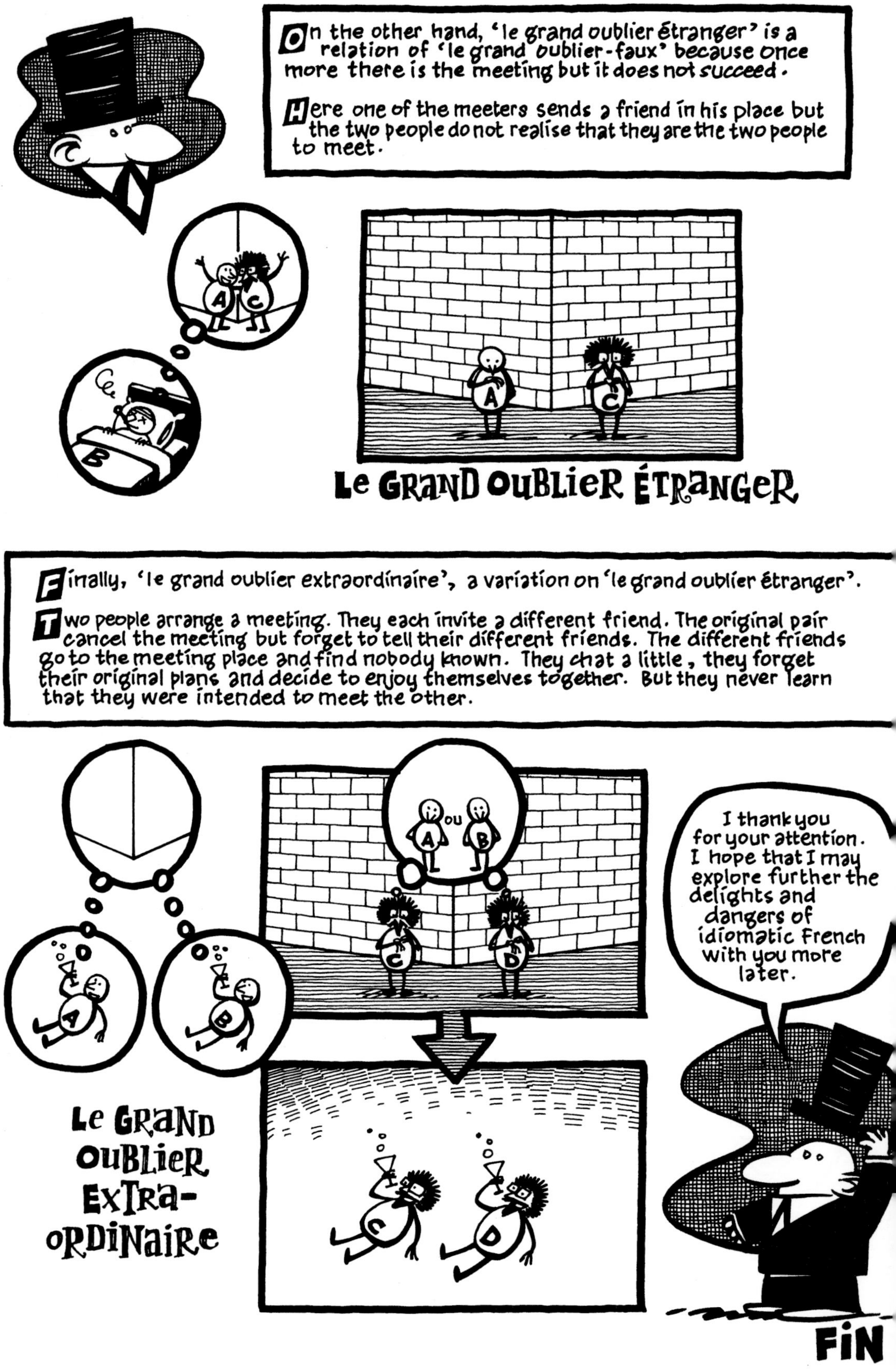
On the other hand, 'le grand oublier étranger' is a relation of 'le grand oublier-faux' because once more there is the meeting but it does not succeed.
Here one of the meeters sends a friend in his place but the two people do not realise that they are the two people to meet.
A
C
B
A
C
Le Grand Oublier Étranger
Finally, 'le grand oublier extraordinaire', a variation on 'le grand oublier étranger'.
Two people arrange a meeting. They each invite a different friend. The original pair cancel the meeting but forget to tell their different friends. The different friends go to the meeting place and find nobody known. They chat a little, they forget their original plans and decide to enjoy themselves together. But they never learn that they were intended to meet the other.
A
B
A
ou
B
C
D
C
D
Le Grand Oublier Extra-ordinaire
I thank you for your attention. I hope that I may explore further the delights and dangers of idiomatic French with you more later.
FIN

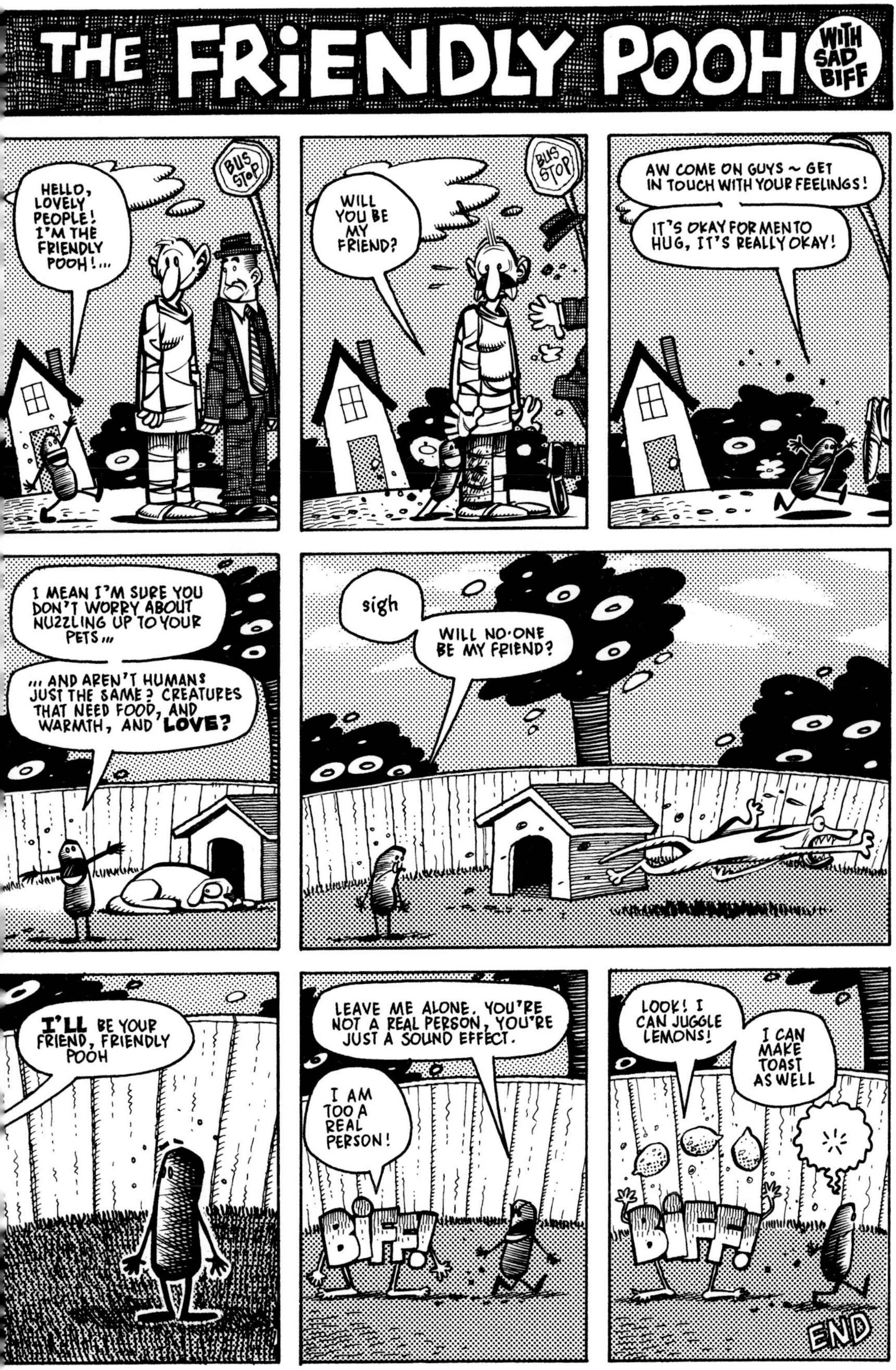

THE FRiENDLY POOH WITH SAD BIFF
BUS STOP
HELLO, LOVELY PEOPLE! I'M THE FRIENDLY POOH!...
WILL YOU BE MY FRIEND?
AW COME ON GUYS ~ GET IN TOUCH WITH YOUR FEELINGS!
IT'S OKAY FOR MEN TO HUG, IT'S REALLY OKAY!
I MEAN I'M SURE YOU DON'T WORRY ABOUT NUZZLING UP TO YOUR PETS...
... AND AREN'T HUMANS JUST THE SAME? CREATURES THAT NEED FOOD, AND WARMTH, AND LOVE?
sigh
WILL NO-ONE BE MY FRIEND?
I'LL BE YOUR FRIEND, FRIENDLY POOH
LEAVE ME ALONE. YOU'RE NOT A REAL PERSON, YOU'RE JUST A SOUND EFFECT.
I AM TOO A REAL PERSON!
BIFF!
LOOK! I CAN JUGGLE LEMONS!
I CAN MAKE TOAST AS WELL
BIFF!
END

The JOURNEY HALFWAY 2

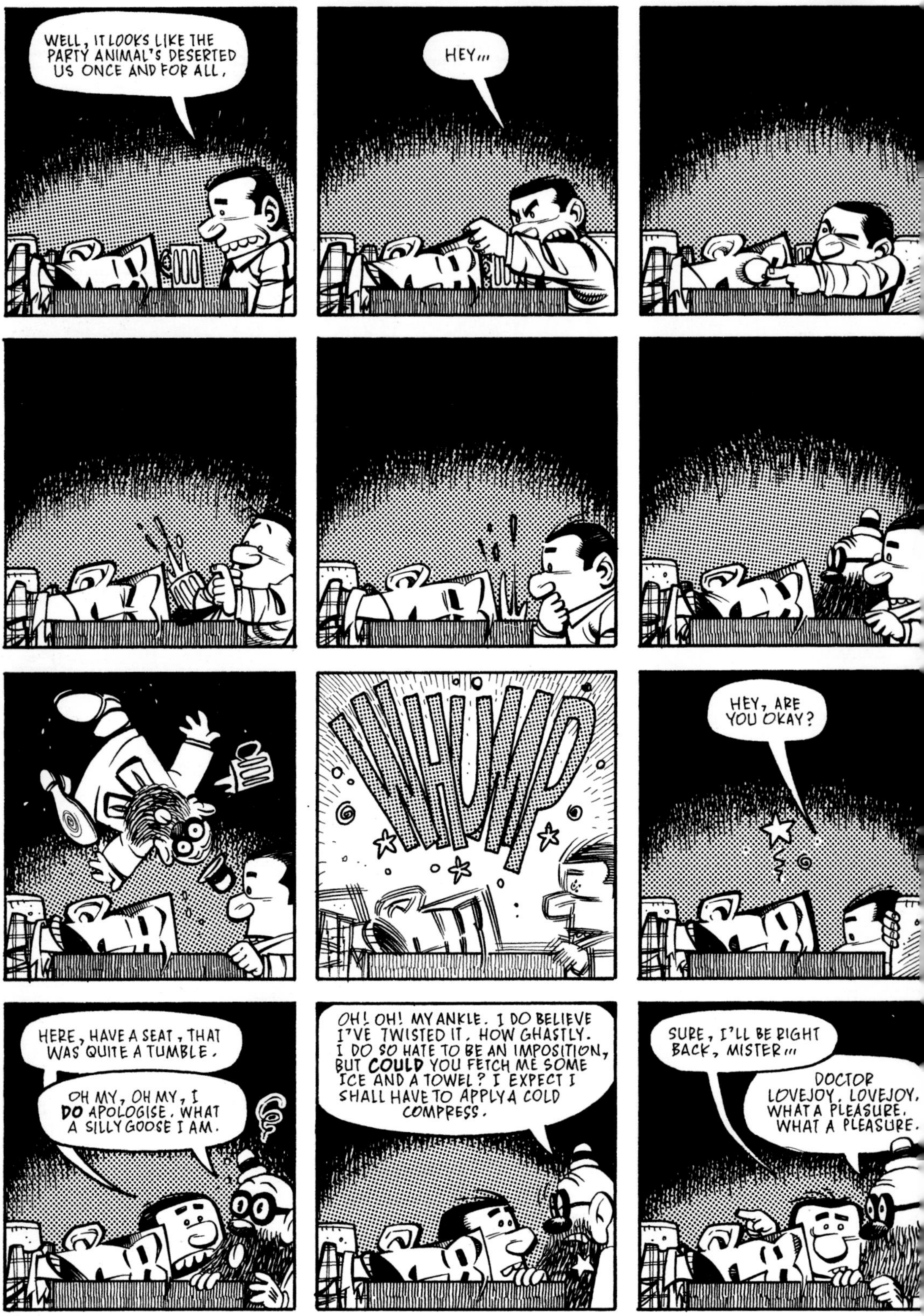
WELL, IT LOOKS LIKE THE PARTY ANIMAL'S DESERTED US ONCE AND FOR ALL.
HEY...
WHUMP
HEY, ARE YOU OKAY?
HERE, HAVE A SEAT, THAT WAS QUITE A TUMBLE.
OH MY, OH MY, I DO APOLOGISE. WHAT A SILLY GOOSE I AM.
OH! OH! MY ANKLE. I DO BELIEVE I'VE TWISTED IT. HOW GHASTLY. I DO SO HATE TO BE AN IMPOSITION, BUT COULD YOU FETCH ME SOME ICE AND A TOWEL? I EXPECT I SHALL HAVE TO APPLY A COLD COMPRESS.
SURE, I'LL BE RIGHT BACK, MISTER...
DOCTOR LOVEJOY. LOVEJOY. WHAT A PLEASURE. WHAT A PLEASURE.

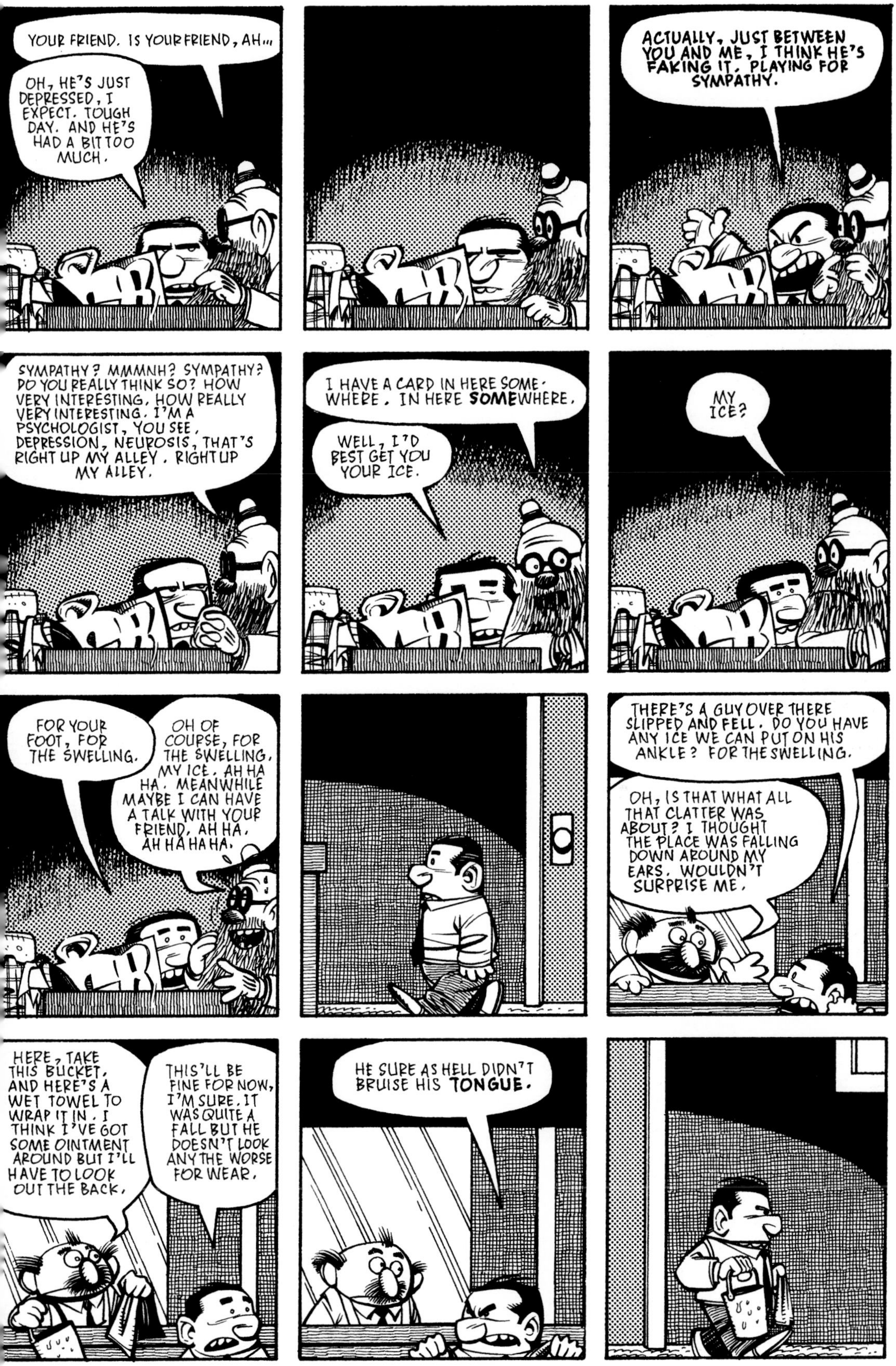
YOUR FRIEND. IS YOUR FRIEND, AH...
OH, HE'S JUST DEPRESSED, I EXPECT. TOUGH DAY. AND HE'S HAD A BIT TOO MUCH.
ACTUALLY, JUST BETWEEN YOU AND ME, I THINK HE'S FAKING IT. PLAYING FOR SYMPATHY.
SYMPATHY? MMMNH? SYMPATHY? DO YOU REALLY THINK SO? HOW VERY INTERESTING. HOW REALLY VERY INTERESTING. I'M A PSYCHOLOGIST, YOU SEE. DEPRESSION, NEUROSIS, THAT'S RIGHT UP MY ALLEY. RIGHT UP MY ALLEY.
I HAVE A CARD IN HERE SOME-WHERE. IN HERE SOMEWHERE.
WELL, I'D BEST GET YOU YOUR ICE.
MY ICE?
FOR YOUR FOOT, FOR THE SWELLING.
OH OF COURSE, FOR THE SWELLING. MY ICE. AH HA HA. MEANWHILE MAYBE I CAN HAVE A TALK WITH YOUR FRIEND, AH HA, AH HA HA HA.
THERE'S A GUY OVER THERE SLIPPED AND FELL. DO YOU HAVE ANY ICE WE CAN PUT ON HIS ANKLE? FOR THE SWELLING.
OH, IS THAT WHAT ALL THAT CLATTER WAS ABOUT? I THOUGHT THE PLACE WAS FALLING DOWN AROUND MY EARS. WOULDN'T SURPRISE ME.
HERE, TAKE THIS BUCKET, AND HERE'S A WET TOWEL TO WRAP IT IN. I THINK I'VE GOT SOME OINTMENT AROUND BUT I'LL HAVE TO LOOK OUT THE BACK.
THIS'LL BE FINE FOR NOW, I'M SURE. IT WAS QUITE A FALL BUT HE DOESN'T LOOK ANY THE WORSE FOR WEAR.
HE SURE AS HELL DIDN'T BRUISE HIS TONGUE.

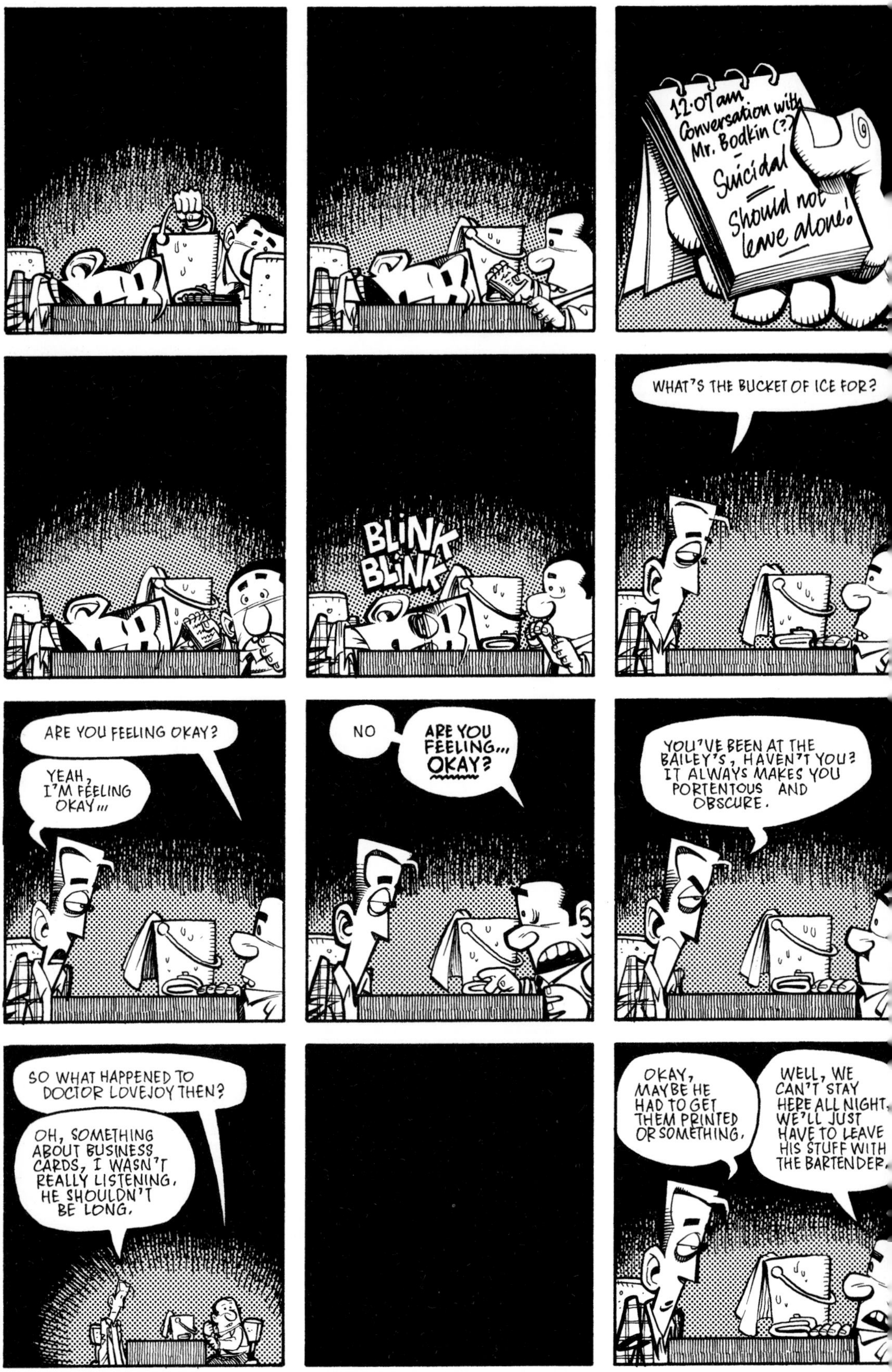
12:07 am
Conversation with Mr. Bodkin (?)
Suicidal
Should not leave alone!
BLINK
BLINK
WHAT'S THE BUCKET OF ICE FOR?
ARE YOU FEELING OKAY?
YEAH, I'M FEELING OKAY...
NO
ARE YOU FEELING... OKAY?
YOU'VE BEEN AT THE BAILEY'S, HAVEN'T YOU? IT ALWAYS MAKES YOU PORTENTOUS AND OBSCURE.
SO WHAT HAPPENED TO DOCTOR LOVEJOY THEN?
OH, SOMETHING ABOUT BUSINESS CARDS, I WASN'T REALLY LISTENING. HE SHOULDN'T BE LONG.
OKAY, MAYBE HE HAD TO GET THEM PRINTED OR SOMETHING.
WELL, WE CAN'T STAY HERE ALL NIGHT. WE'LL JUST HAVE TO LEAVE HIS STUFF WITH THE BARTENDER.

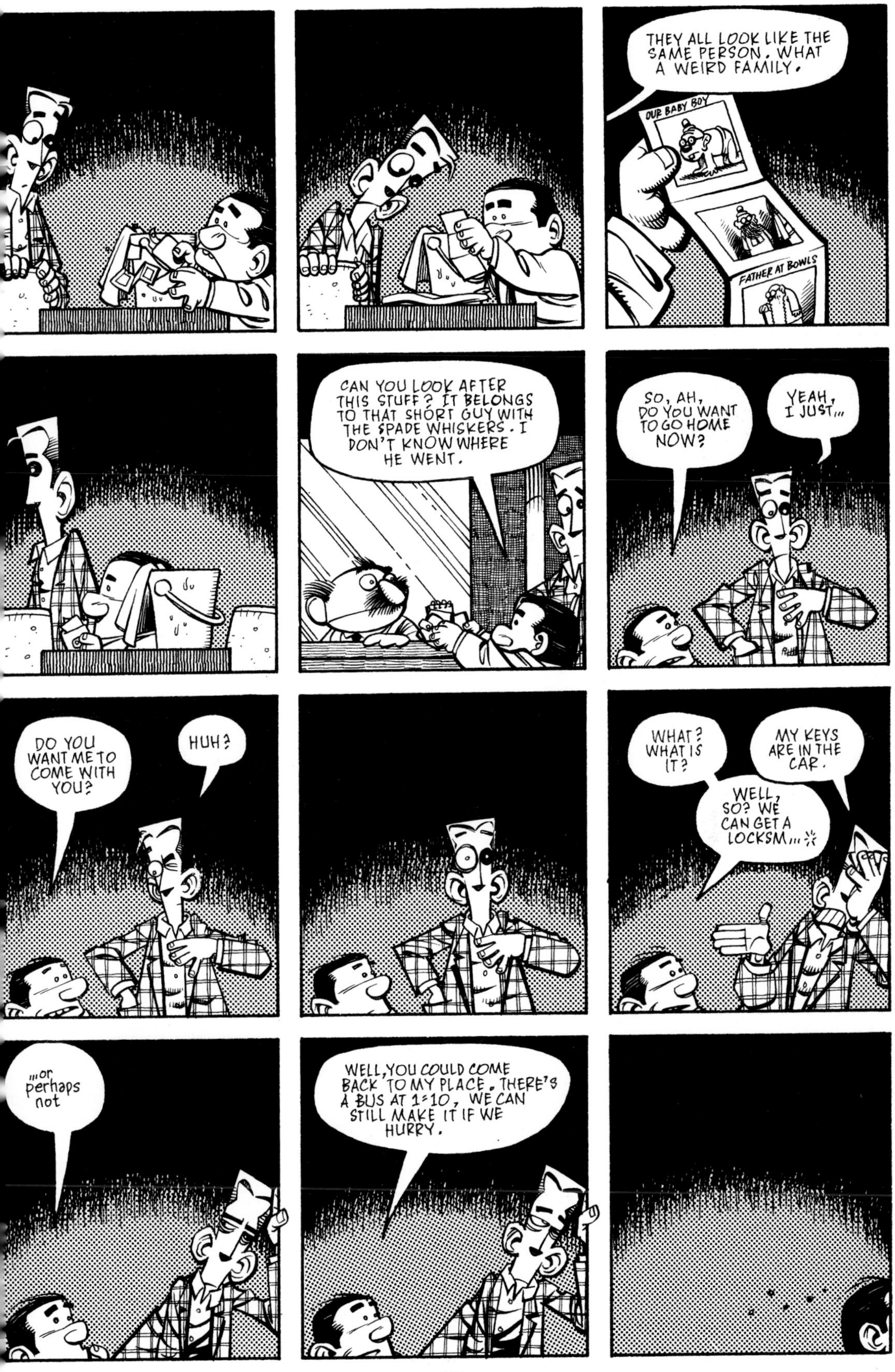

THEY ALL LOOK LIKE THE SAME PERSON. WHAT A WEIRD FAMILY.
OUR BABY BOY
FATHER AT BOWLS
CAN YOU LOOK AFTER THIS STUFF? IT BELONGS TO THAT SHORT GUY WITH THE SPADE WHISKERS. I DON'T KNOW WHERE HE WENT.
SO, AH, DO YOU WANT TO GO HOME NOW?
YEAH, I JUST...
DO YOU WANT ME TO COME WITH YOU?
HUH?
WHAT? WHAT IS IT?
MY KEYS ARE IN THE CAR.
WELL, SO? WE CAN GET A LOCKSM...
...or perhaps not
WELL, YOU COULD COME BACK TO MY PLACE. THERE'S A BUS AT 1:10, WE CAN STILL MAKE IT IF WE HURRY.

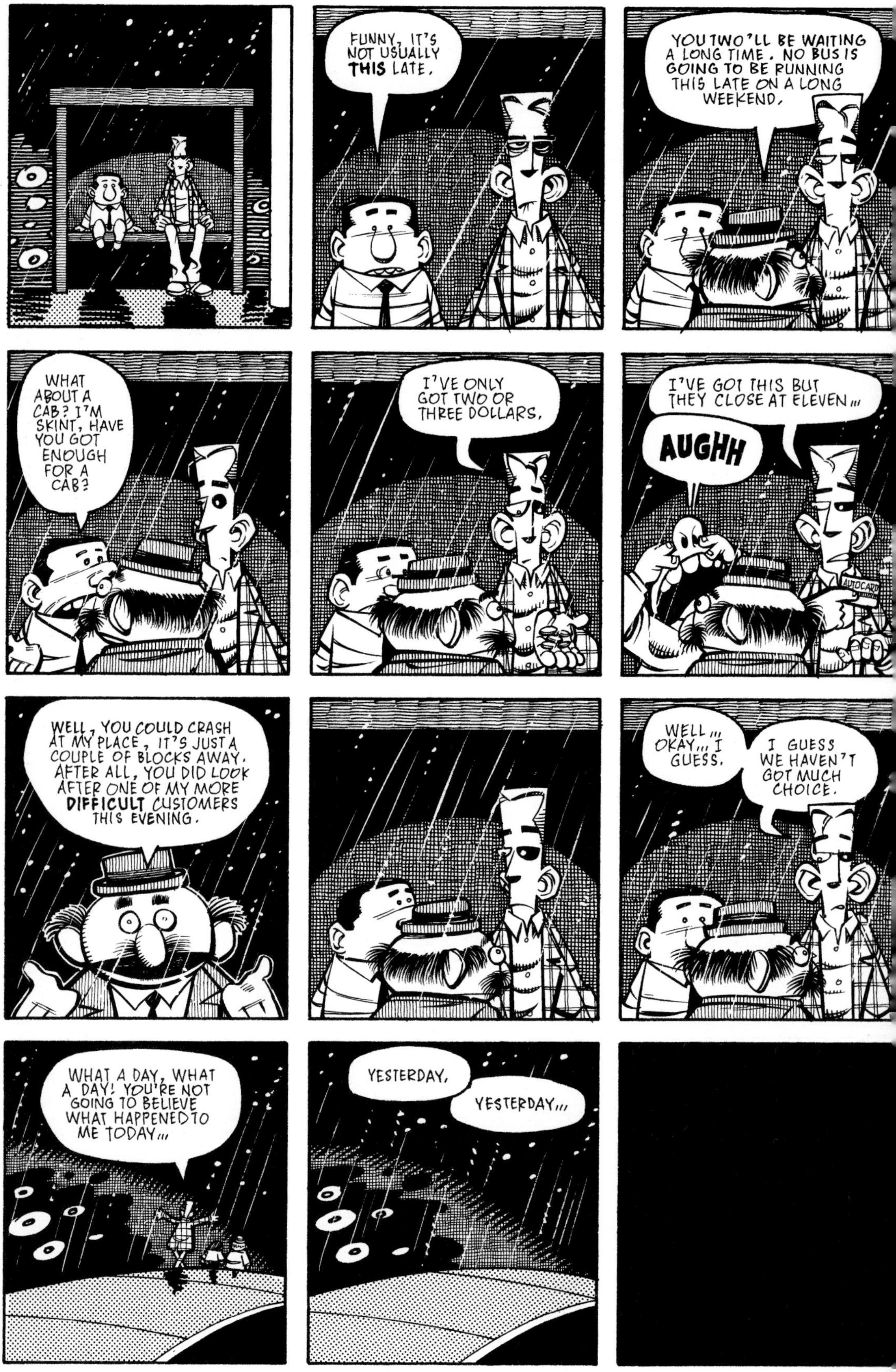
FUNNY, IT'S NOT USUALLY **THIS** LATE.
YOU TWO'LL BE WAITING A LONG TIME. NO BUS IS GOING TO BE RUNNING THIS LATE ON A LONG WEEKEND.
WHAT ABOUT A CAB? I'M SKINT, HAVE YOU GOT ENOUGH FOR A CAB?
I'VE ONLY GOT TWO OR THREE DOLLARS.
I'VE GOT THIS BUT THEY CLOSE AT ELEVEN...
AUGHH
AUTOCARD
WELL, YOU COULD CRASH AT MY PLACE, IT'S JUST A COUPLE OF BLOCKS AWAY. AFTER ALL, YOU DID LOOK AFTER ONE OF MY MORE **DIFFICULT** CUSTOMERS THIS EVENING.
WELL... OKAY... I GUESS.
I GUESS WE HAVEN'T GOT MUCH CHOICE.
WHAT A DAY, WHAT A DAY! YOU'RE NOT GOING TO BELIEVE WHAT HAPPENED TO ME TODAY...
YESTERDAY.
YESTERDAY...

WE REGRET THAT OUR REGULARLY SCHEDULED EPISODE OF **LIFESTYLES OF THE RICH AND CHURLISH** HAS HAD TO BE CANCELLED OUT OF SPITE.

EMON ARANGUE PIE

WITH THE **GUMP**

OH NO YOU DON'T.

IF YOU'RE GOING TO EAT ME YOU'RE GOING TO DO IT WITH **CLEAN FINGERNAILS**

NOW YOU GO AND CLEAN THOSE FINGERNAILS. AND MAKE SURE YOU DO BOTH HANDS BECAUSE I'LL BE CHECKING!

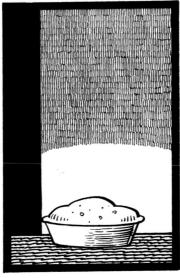

AND TUCK THAT SHIRT IN!

AL RL 92

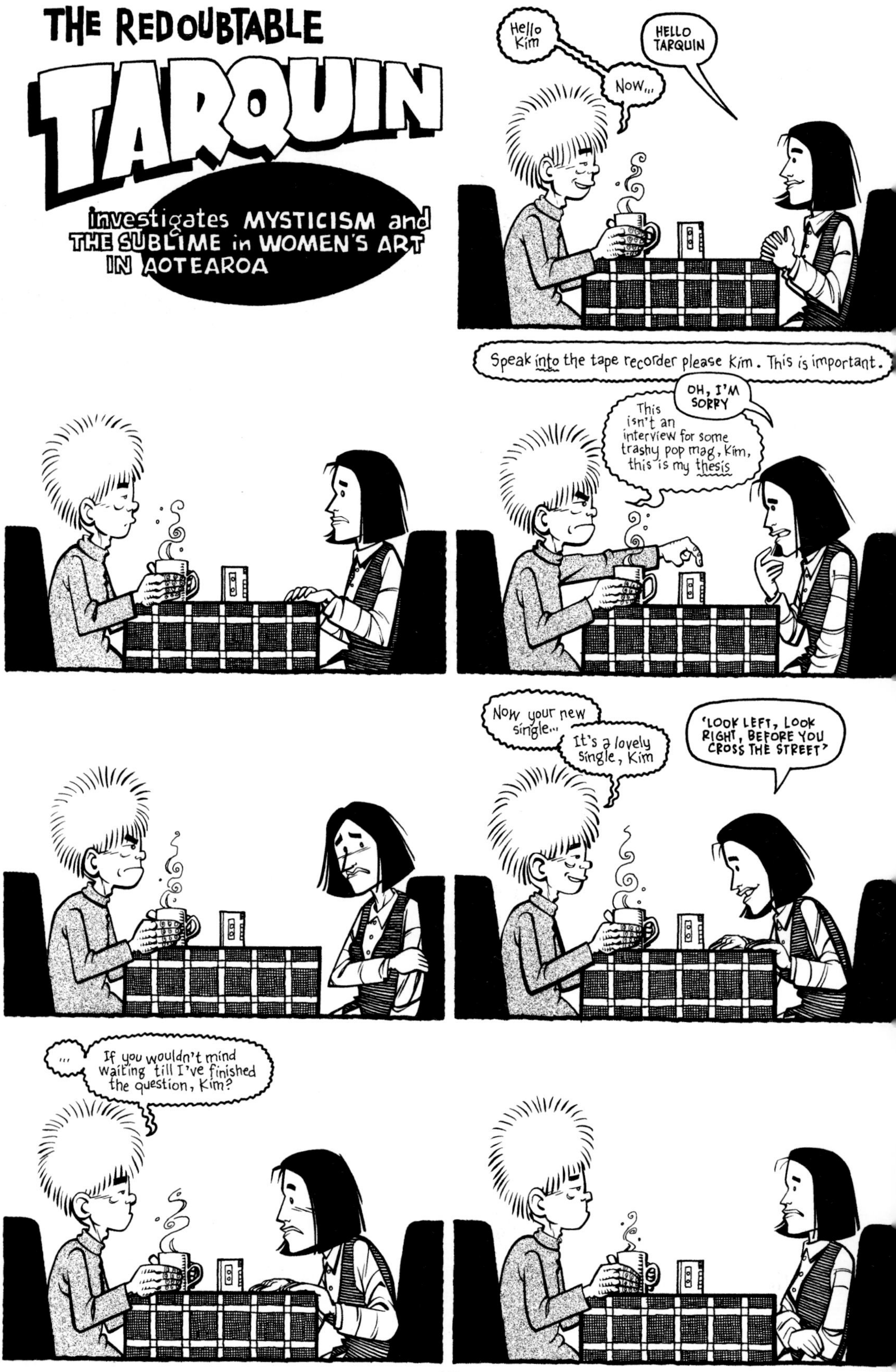
THE REDOUBTABLE
TARQUIN
investigates MYSTICISM and THE SUBLIME in WOMEN'S ART IN AOTEAROA
Hello Kim
Now...
HELLO TARQUIN
Speak into the tape recorder please Kim. This is important.
This isn't an interview for some trashy pop mag, Kim, this is my thesis
OH, I'M SORRY
Now your new single...
It's a lovely single, Kim
'LOOK LEFT, LOOK RIGHT, BEFORE YOU CROSS THE STREET'
...
If you wouldn't mind waiting till I've finished the question, Kim?

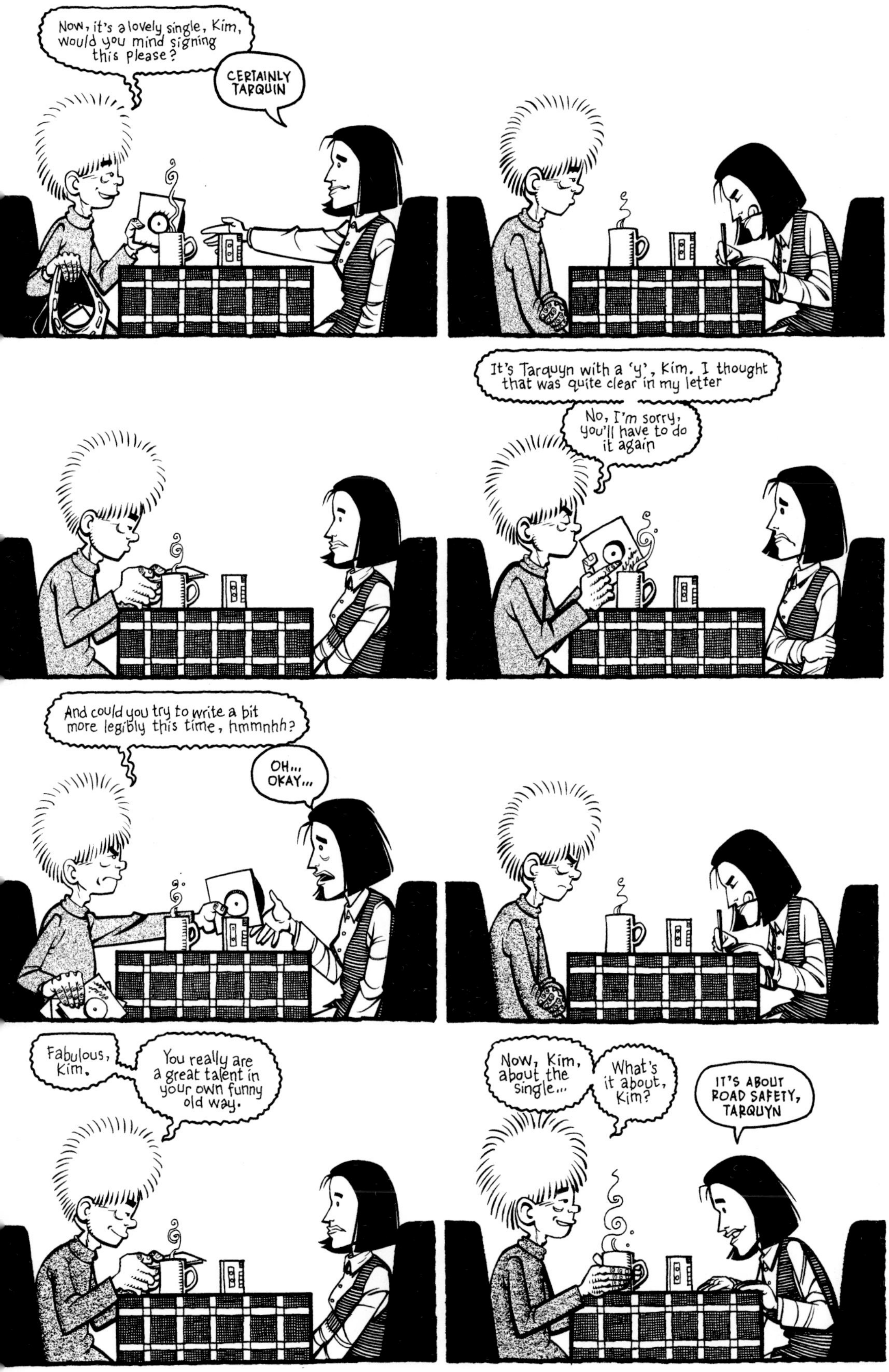
Now, it's a lovely single, Kim, would you mind signing this please?
CERTAINLY TARQUIN
It's Tarquyn with a 'y', Kim. I thought that was quite clear in my letter
No, I'm sorry, you'll have to do it again
And could you try to write a bit more legibly this time, hmmnhh?
OH... OKAY...
Fabulous, Kim.
You really are a great talent in your own funny old way.
Now, Kim, about the single...
What's it about, Kim?
IT'S ABOUT ROAD SAFETY, TARQUYN

Think very carefully
IT IS ABOUT ROAD SAFETY, TARQUYN
You're not being very cooperative Kim
BUT TARQUYN...
Mysticism. And. The. Sublime. Kim. That's what it's all about.
I hope you don't have anything on tonight, Kim, because I'm prepared to sit this one out if need be...
WELL, I SUPPOSE THERE MIGHT BE SOMETHING ABOUT MYTH AND RITUAL IN THERE SOMEWHERE.
"Mysticism and the sublime"
... MYSTICISM AND THE SUBLIME.
There, that wasn't so difficult now, wasn't it?
Sigh

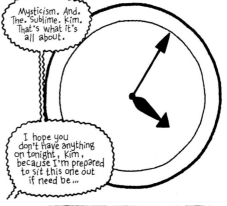

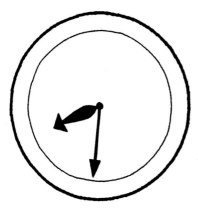

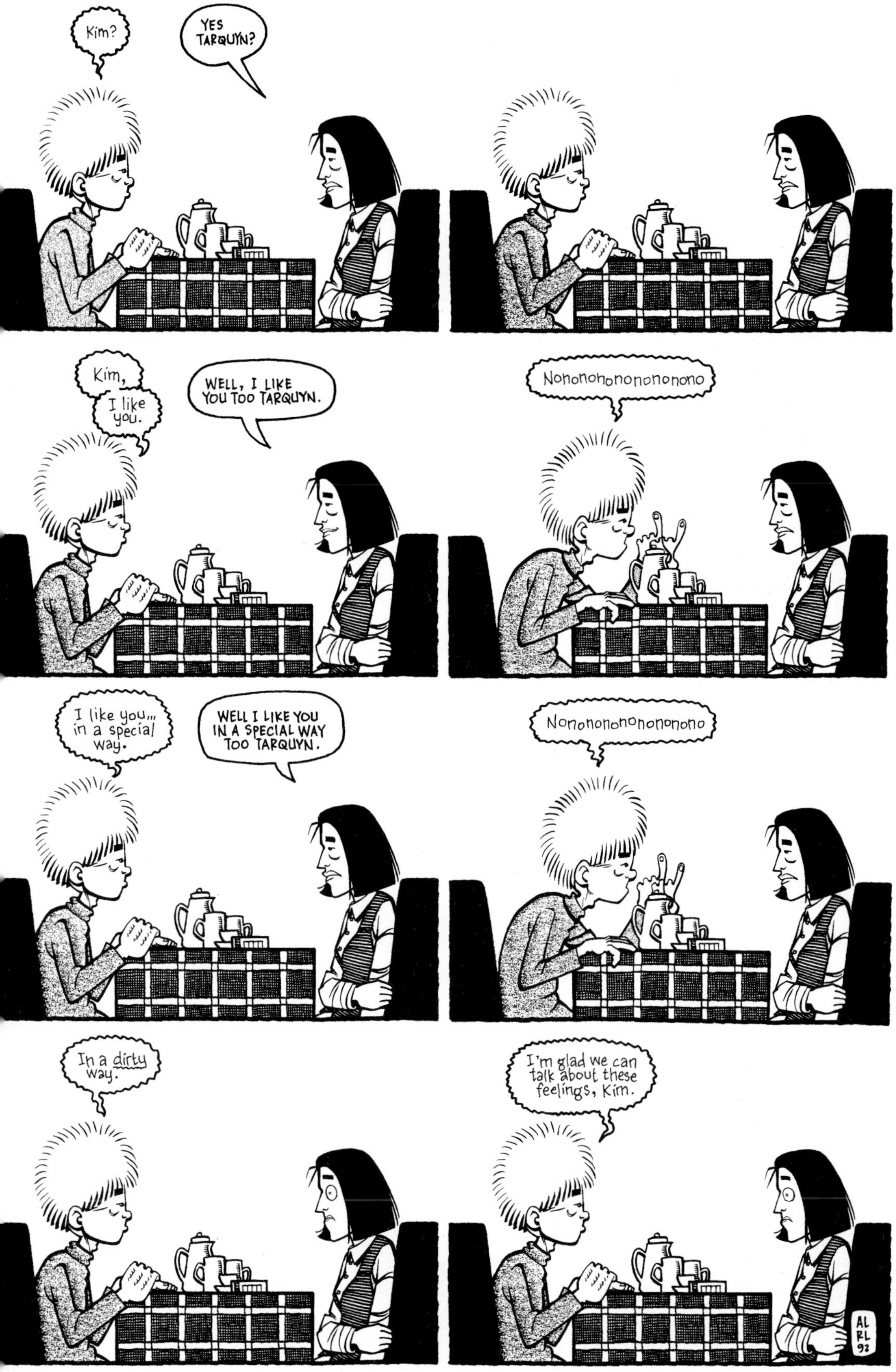
Kim?
YES TARQUYN?
Kim,
I like you.
WELL, I LIKE YOU TOO TARQUYN.
Nononohononononono
I like you... in a special way.
WELL I LIKE YOU IN A SPECIAL WAY TOO TARQUYN.
Nononononononononono
In a dirty way.
I'm glad we can talk about these feelings, Kim.
AL RL 92

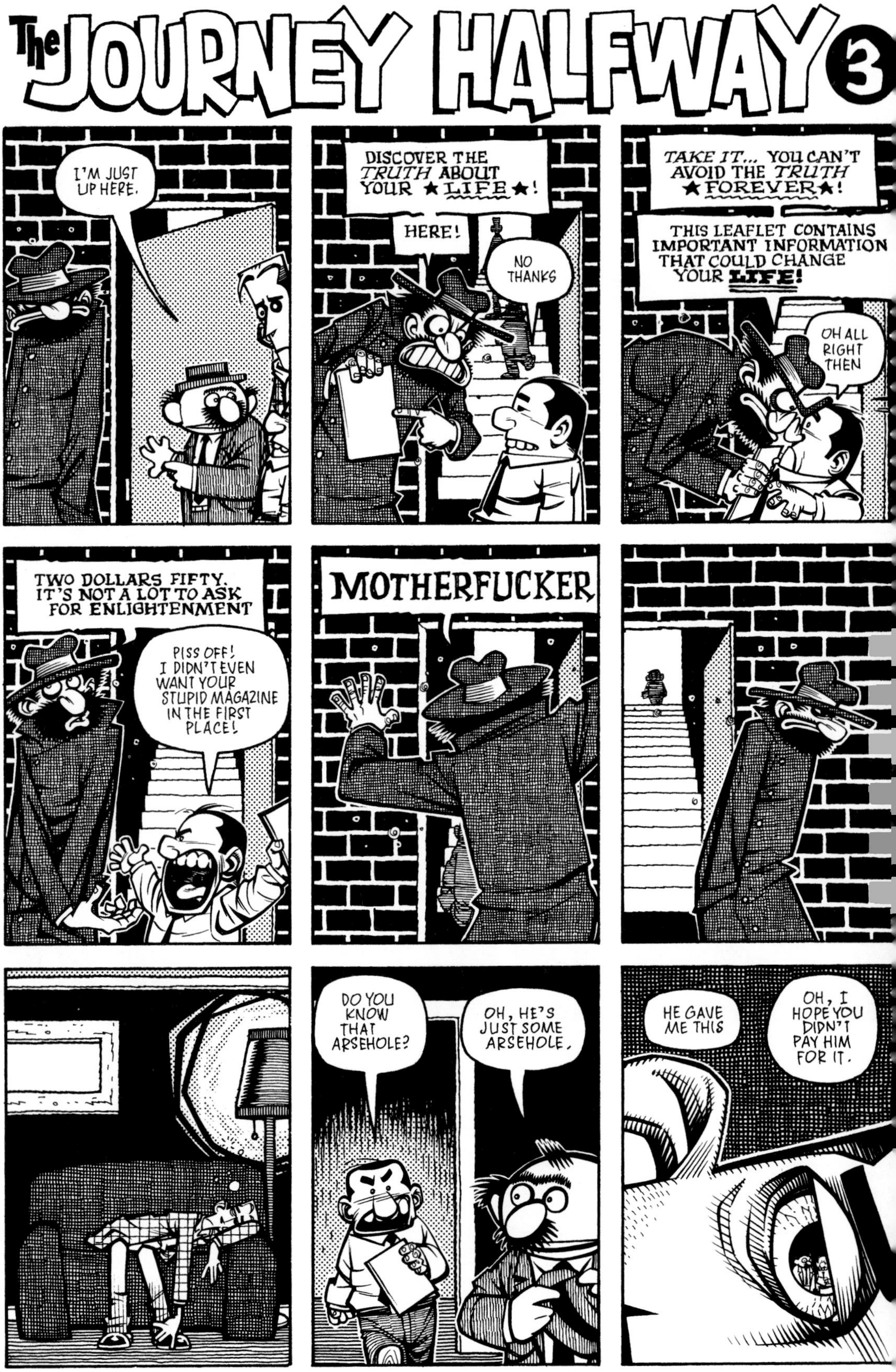
The JOURNEY HALFWAY 3
I'M JUST UP HERE.
DISCOVER THE TRUTH ABOUT YOUR ★LIFE★!
HERE!
NO THANKS
TAKE IT... YOU CAN'T AVOID THE TRUTH ★FOREVER★!
THIS LEAFLET CONTAINS IMPORTANT INFORMATION THAT COULD CHANGE YOUR LIFE!
OH ALL RIGHT THEN
TWO DOLLARS FIFTY. IT'S NOT A LOT TO ASK FOR ENLIGHTENMENT
PISS OFF! I DIDN'T EVEN WANT YOUR STUPID MAGAZINE IN THE FIRST PLACE!
MOTHERFUCKER
DO YOU KNOW THAT ARSEHOLE?
OH, HE'S JUST SOME ARSEHOLE.
HE GAVE ME THIS
OH, I HOPE YOU DIDN'T PAY HIM FOR IT.

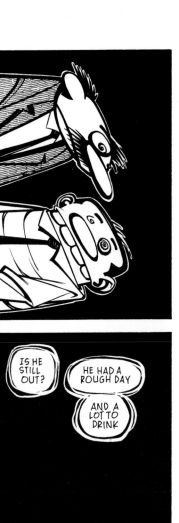

GOOD.

IS HE STILL OUT?

HE HAD A ROUGH DAY

AND A LOT TO DRINK

I MEAN, WHAT AN ARSEHOLE. *THE PERILS OF INTERMARRIAGE* BY *MR. LARRY HERBERT ESQ.*

"THE MOREL DECLINE," MORAL WITH AN *E*, "OF SOCIETY IS MOST MARKED IN THE WIDESPREAD INFECTION OF THE EPIDEMIC ★*MISCEGENATION*★!"

AN ARSEHOLE, LIKE I SAID. WHAT CAN YOU DO?

WELL, I'LL HAVE TO GO NOW. IT'LL LOCK BEHIND YOU. PULL IT FIRMLY TO BE SURE AND MAYBE I'LL SEE YOU THERE LATER.

I DON'T KNOW YET. YOU DON'T HAVE A SMALL HAND MIRROR, DO YOU?

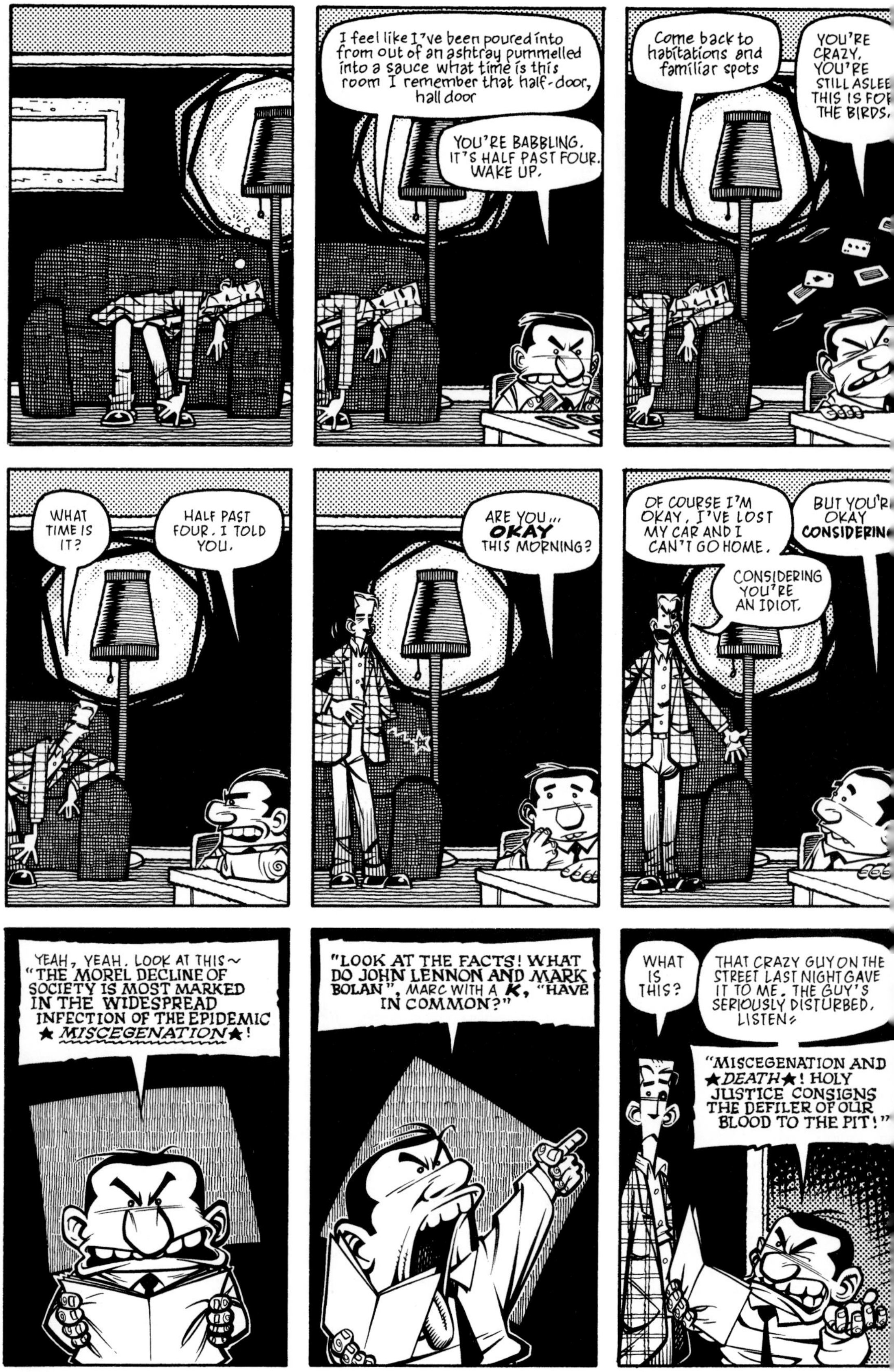
I feel like I've been poured into from out of an ashtray pummelled into a sauce what time is this room I remember that half-door, hall door
YOU'RE BABBLING. IT'S HALF PAST FOUR. WAKE UP.
Come back to habitations and familiar spots
YOU'RE CRAZY, YOU'RE STILL ASLEE THIS IS FOR THE BIRDS.
WHAT TIME IS IT?
HALF PAST FOUR. I TOLD YOU.
ARE YOU... OKAY THIS MORNING?
OF COURSE I'M OKAY, I'VE LOST MY CAR AND I CAN'T GO HOME.
BUT YOU'R OKAY CONSIDERIN
CONSIDERING YOU'RE AN IDIOT.
YEAH, YEAH. LOOK AT THIS~ "THE MOREL DECLINE OF SOCIETY IS MOST MARKED IN THE WIDESPREAD INFECTION OF THE EPIDEMIC ★ MISCEGENATION ★!
"LOOK AT THE FACTS! WHAT DO JOHN LENNON AND MARK BOLAN", MARC WITH A K, "HAVE IN COMMON?"
WHAT IS THIS?
THAT CRAZY GUY ON THE STREET LAST NIGHT GAVE IT TO ME. THE GUY'S SERIOUSLY DISTURBED. LISTEN:
"MISCEGENATION AND ★ DEATH ★! HOLY JUSTICE CONSIGNS THE DEFILER OF OUR BLOOD TO THE PIT!"

SOMETHING, SOMETHING... UMMM... "THE SONS OF"... NO...

"WHAT EVER HAPPENED TO DECENT LAD-AND-GIRL LOVE? WHEN THE LILYWHITE VIRGIN MARRIES THE *COONS'* BLACK AS COAL THERE BEGINS A BATTLE BETWEEN THE HUSBAND AND WIFE ~ A *FEARFUL, BLOODY* BATTLE THAT CAN END ONLY WITH THE *DEATH* OF ONE. THE SACRED COMPACT OF MATRIMONY CANNOT WITHSTAND..."

CAN YOU **BELIEVE** THIS GUY?! IF HE'S STILL THERE WHEN WE GO I'LL SMASH HIS SICK FACE IN, OR BREAK HIS FINGERS, AT LEAST.

OH, WHY BOTHER?

HERE: "ONCE WE CONTENANCE (CONTENANCE!) MARRIAGE OUTSIDE ONES RACE (*NO APOSTROPHE*) THEN ANY MANNER OF DEPRAVITY IS POSSIBLE ~ MATINGS ACROSS THE NATURAL BOUNDARIES OF CLASS OR GENDER OR SPECIES!! THE PROBLEMS WILL BE CLEAR IN THE CHILDREN OF SUCH LUSTFUL FORNICATION.

"THE SCANDAL HAS HIT EVEN OUR ROYAL FAMILY. THE LADY WHO ALLOWS HERSELF TO BE DEFILED, SHE IS NO BETTER THAN HER MAN. TO DESTROY THE HOUSE OF WINDSOR IN THIS MANNER OUGHT TO BE A *CAPITAL OFFENCE.* AND INDEED! LOOK TO THE CONSEQUENCES! SHE NEVER KNEW THE WORST, BECAUSE SHE DIED IN GIVING BIRTH, BUT NOW SHE KNOWS IT ALL, BEING DEAD." ~ *MR. LARRY HERBERT ESQ. BORN WHITE, 1939.*

AN AUSPICIOUS YEAR.

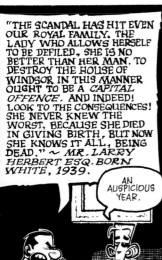

IS IT AFTER SIX YET?

YES, WHY?

WE HAVE TO LEAVE. I'VE BEEN THINKING AND THERE'S SOMETHING I HAVE TO FIND OUT.

WHERE ARE WE GOING?

WE'RE GOING TO THE THEATRE.

DON'T LOOK AT ME LIKE THAT.

END CHAPTER THREE

43

Calling Claire: HOUR ONE

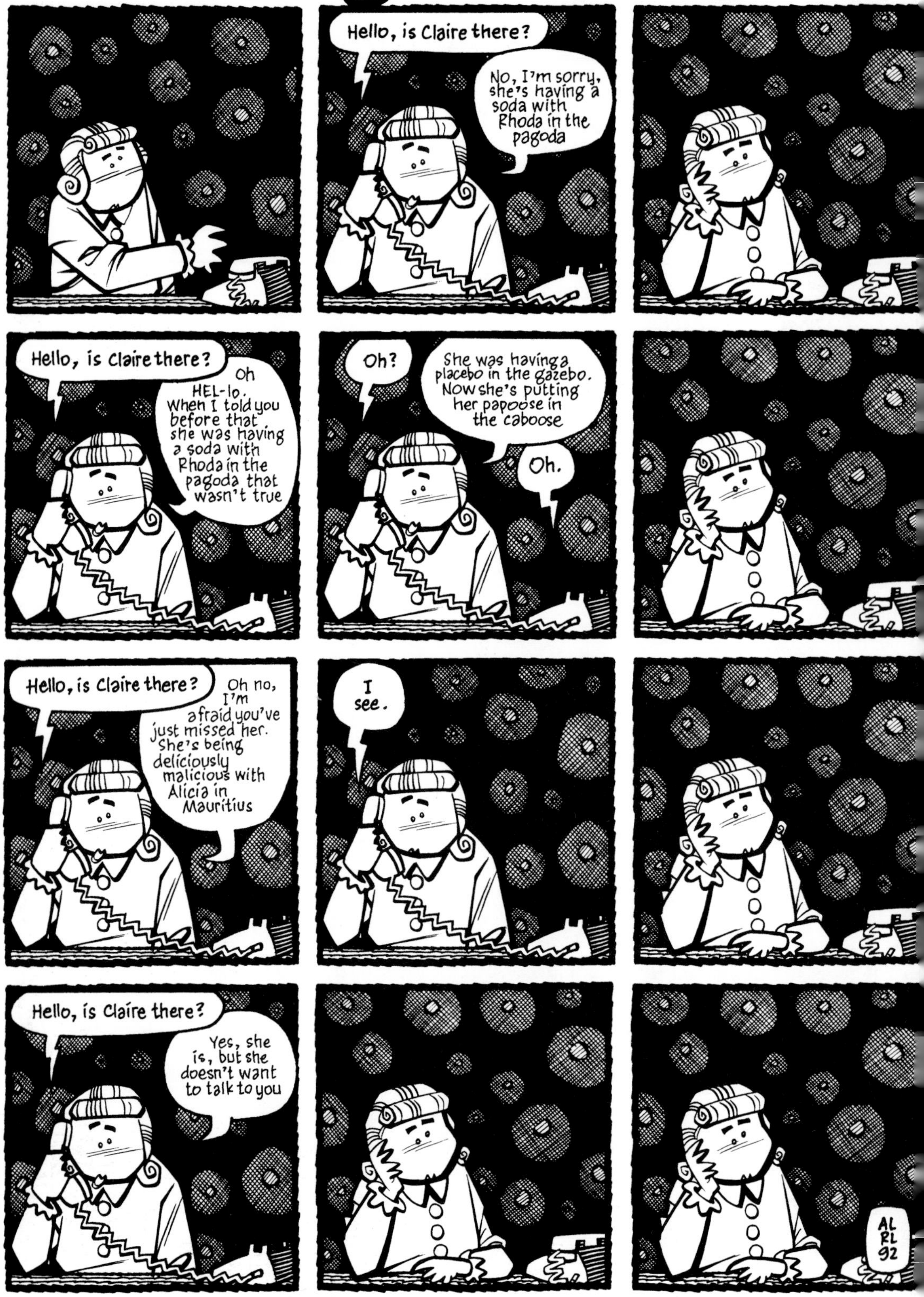
Hello, is Claire there?
No, I'm sorry, she's having a soda with Rhoda in the pagoda
Hello, is Claire there?
Oh HEL-lo. When I told you before that she was having a soda with Rhoda in the pagoda that wasn't true
Oh?
She was having a placebo in the gazebo. Now she's putting her papoose in the caboose
Oh.
Hello, is Claire there?
Oh no, I'm afraid you've just missed her. She's being deliciously malicious with Alicia in Mauritius
I see.
Hello, is Claire there?
Yes, she is, but she doesn't want to talk to you
AL RL 92

LAUGH! WITH THOSE WACKY TIME TRAVELLERS

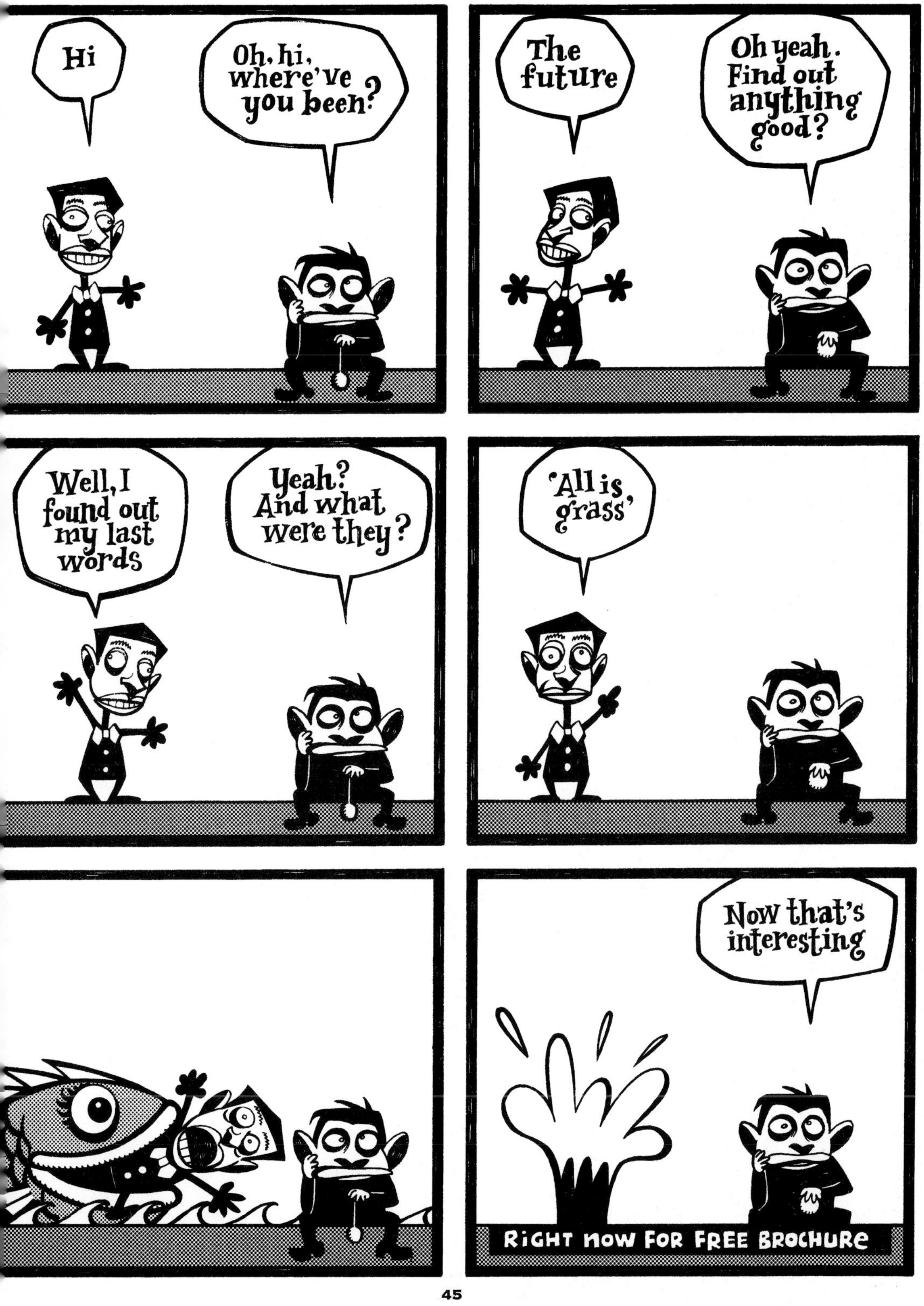

Hi
Oh, hi, where've you been?
The future
Oh yeah. Find out anything good?
Well, I found out my last words
Yeah? And what were they?
'All is grass'
Now that's interesting
RIGHT NOW FOR FREE BROCHURE

The JOURNEY HALFWAY 4

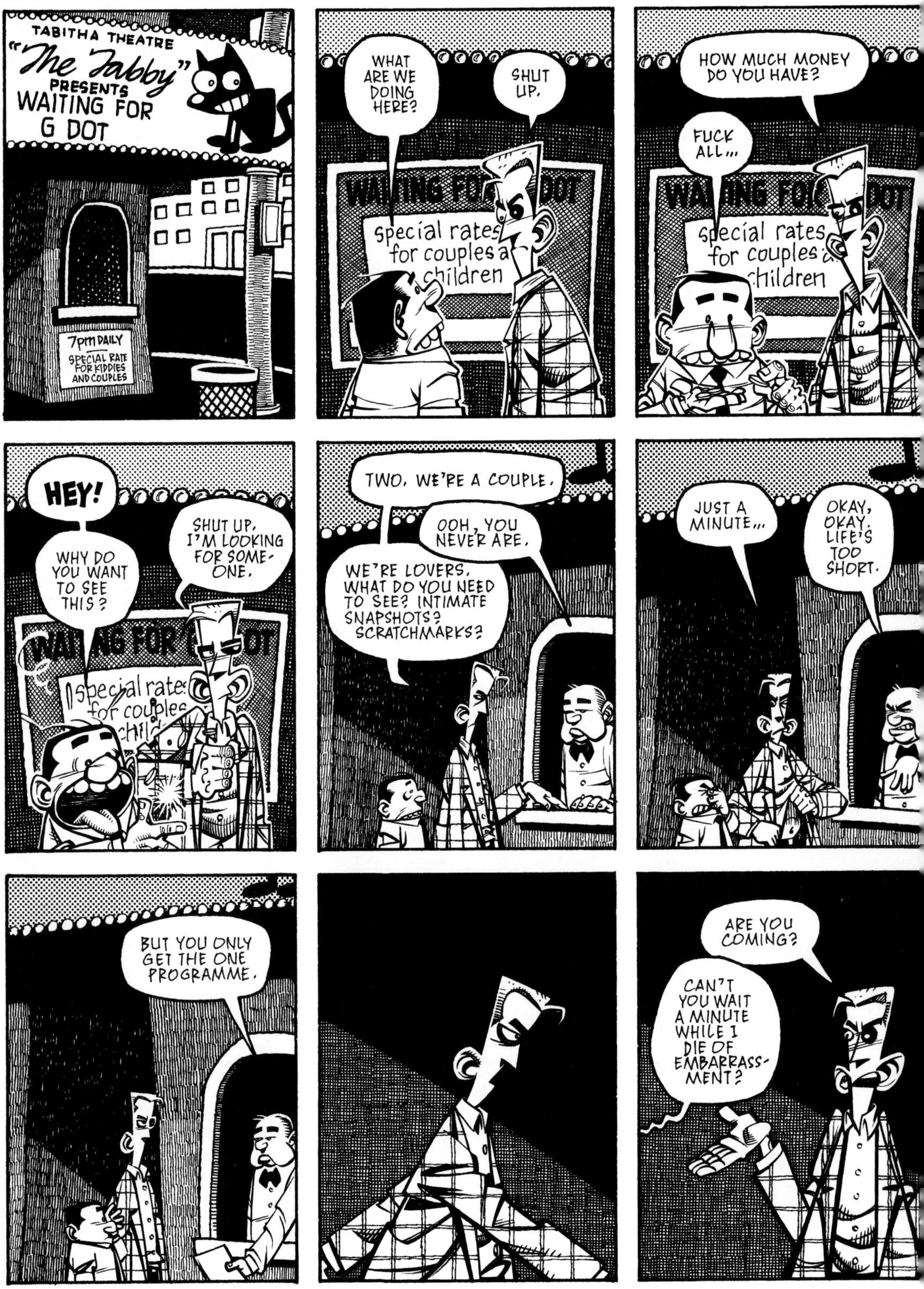
TABITHA THEATRE
"The Tabby" PRESENTS
WAITING FOR G DOT
7pm DAILY
SPECIAL RATE FOR KIDDIES AND COUPLES
WHAT ARE WE DOING HERE?
SHUT UP.
HOW MUCH MONEY DO YOU HAVE?
FUCK ALL...
HEY!
WHY DO YOU WANT TO SEE THIS?
SHUT UP, I'M LOOKING FOR SOME-ONE.
TWO. WE'RE A COUPLE.
OOH, YOU NEVER ARE.
WE'RE LOVERS. WHAT DO YOU NEED TO SEE? INTIMATE SNAPSHOTS? SCRATCHMARKS?
JUST A MINUTE...
OKAY, OKAY. LIFE'S TOO SHORT.
BUT YOU ONLY GET THE ONE PROGRAMME.
ARE YOU COMING?
CAN'T YOU WAIT A MINUTE WHILE I DIE OF EMBARRASS-MENT?

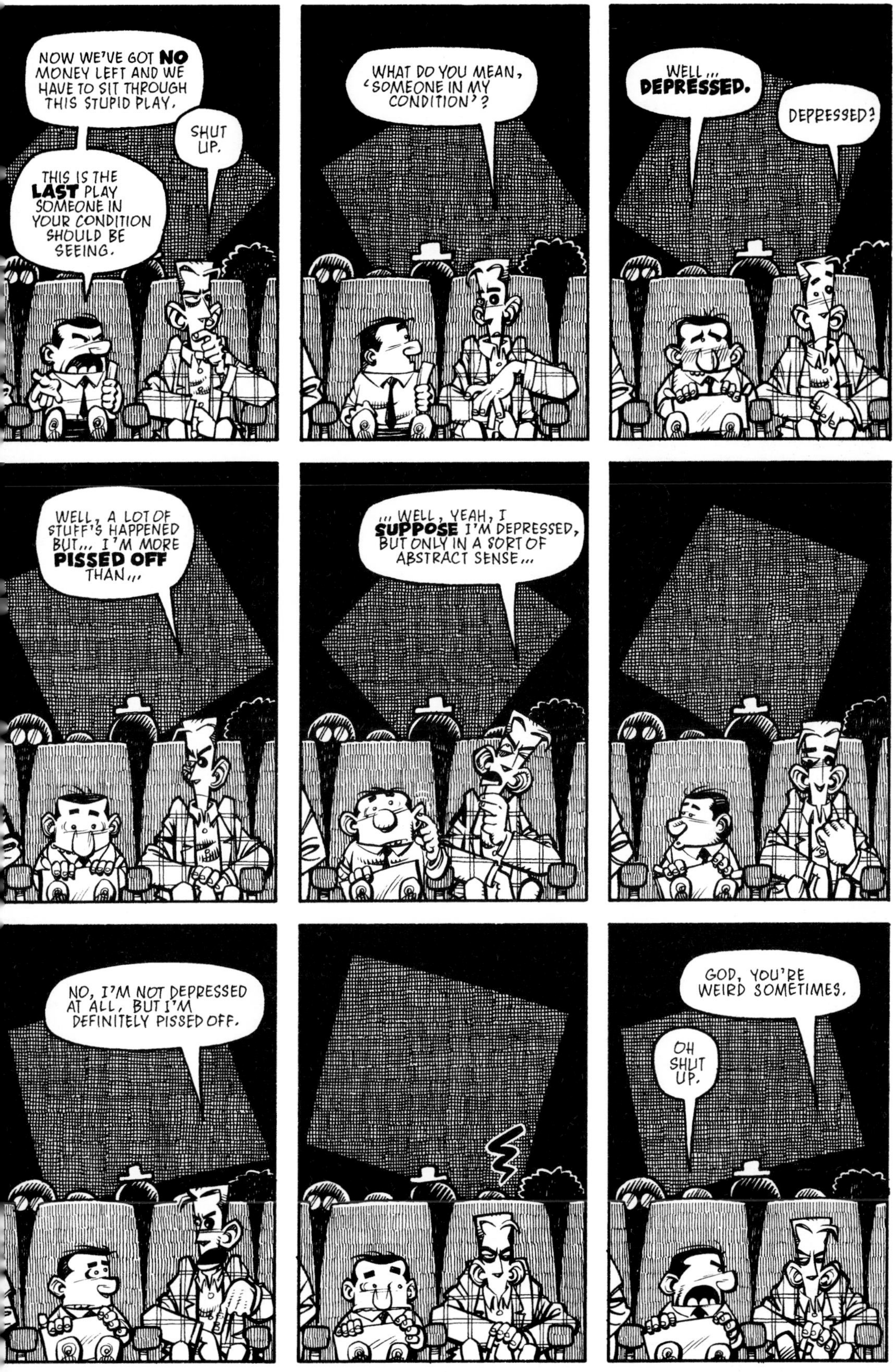
NOW WE'VE GOT **NO** MONEY LEFT AND WE HAVE TO SIT THROUGH THIS STUPID PLAY.
SHUT UP.
THIS IS THE **LAST** PLAY SOMEONE IN YOUR CONDITION SHOULD BE SEEING.
WHAT DO YOU MEAN, 'SOMEONE IN MY CONDITION'?
WELL... **DEPRESSED.**
DEPRESSED?
WELL, A LOT OF STUFF'S HAPPENED BUT... I'M MORE **PISSED OFF** THAN...
...WELL, YEAH, I **SUPPOSE** I'M DEPRESSED, BUT ONLY IN A SORT OF ABSTRACT SENSE...
NO, I'M NOT DEPRESSED AT ALL, BUT I'M DEFINITELY PISSED OFF.
GOD, YOU'RE WEIRD SOMETIMES.
OH SHUT UP.

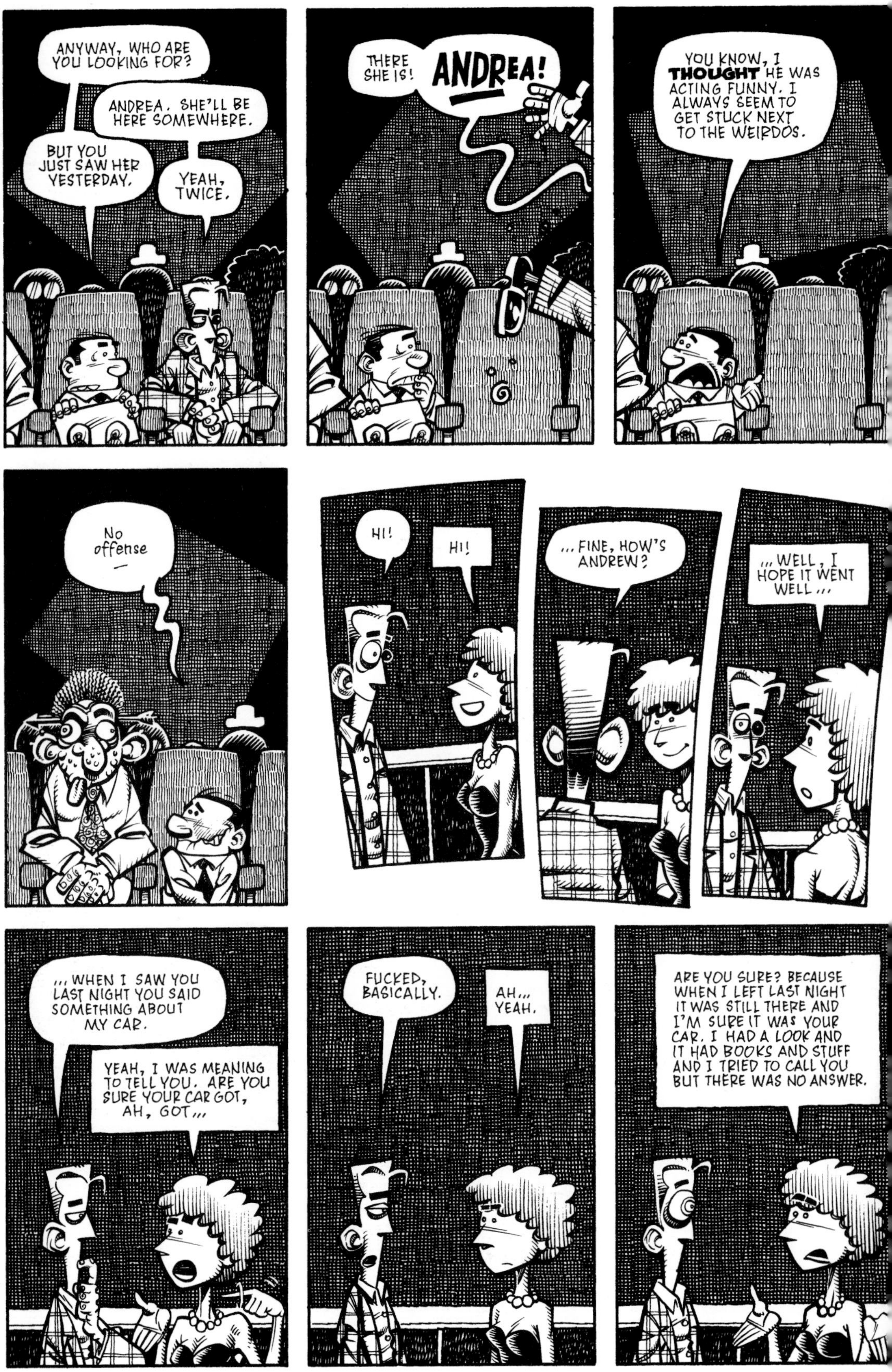
ANYWAY, WHO ARE YOU LOOKING FOR?
ANDREA. SHE'LL BE HERE SOMEWHERE.
BUT YOU JUST SAW HER YESTERDAY.
YEAH, TWICE.
THERE SHE IS!
ANDREA!
YOU KNOW, I THOUGHT HE WAS ACTING FUNNY. I ALWAYS SEEM TO GET STUCK NEXT TO THE WEIRDOS.
No offense
HI!
HI!
... FINE, HOW'S ANDREW?
... WELL, I HOPE IT WENT WELL ...
... WHEN I SAW YOU LAST NIGHT YOU SAID SOMETHING ABOUT MY CAR.
YEAH, I WAS MEANING TO TELL YOU. ARE YOU SURE YOUR CAR GOT, AH, GOT ...
FUCKED, BASICALLY.
AH... YEAH.
ARE YOU SURE? BECAUSE WHEN I LEFT LAST NIGHT IT WAS STILL THERE AND I'M SURE IT WAS YOUR CAR. I HAD A LOOK AND IT HAD BOOKS AND STUFF AND I TRIED TO CALL YOU BUT THERE WAS NO ANSWER.

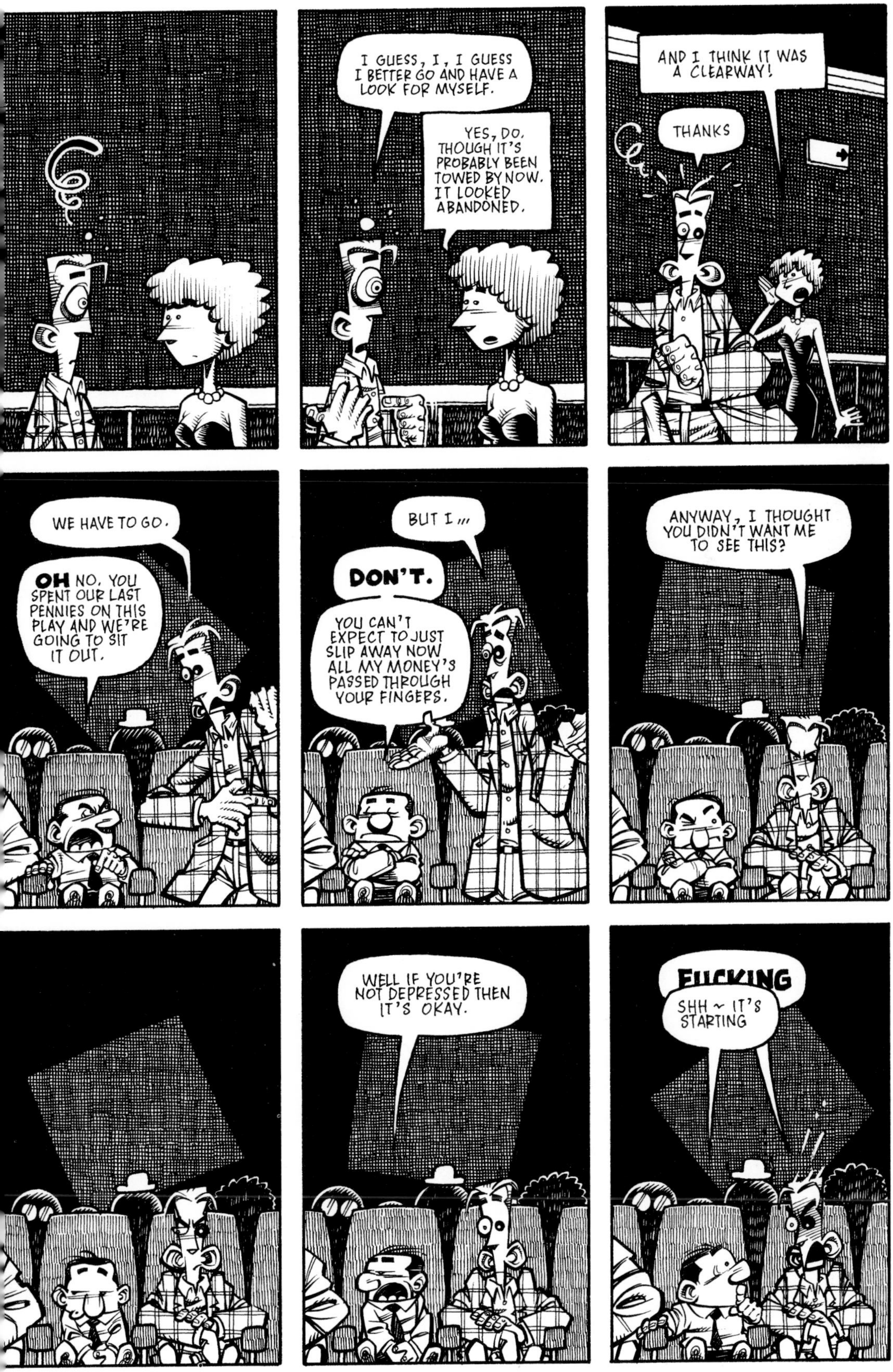
I GUESS, I, I GUESS I BETTER GO AND HAVE A LOOK FOR MYSELF.
YES, DO, THOUGH IT'S PROBABLY BEEN TOWED BY NOW. IT LOOKED ABANDONED.
AND I THINK IT WAS A CLEARWAY!
THANKS
WE HAVE TO GO.
OH NO. YOU SPENT OUR LAST PENNIES ON THIS PLAY AND WE'RE GOING TO SIT IT OUT.
BUT I ...
DON'T.
YOU CAN'T EXPECT TO JUST SLIP AWAY NOW ALL MY MONEY'S PASSED THROUGH YOUR FINGERS.
ANYWAY, I THOUGHT YOU DIDN'T WANT ME TO SEE THIS?
WELL IF YOU'RE NOT DEPRESSED THEN IT'S OKAY.
FUCKING
SHH ~ IT'S STARTING

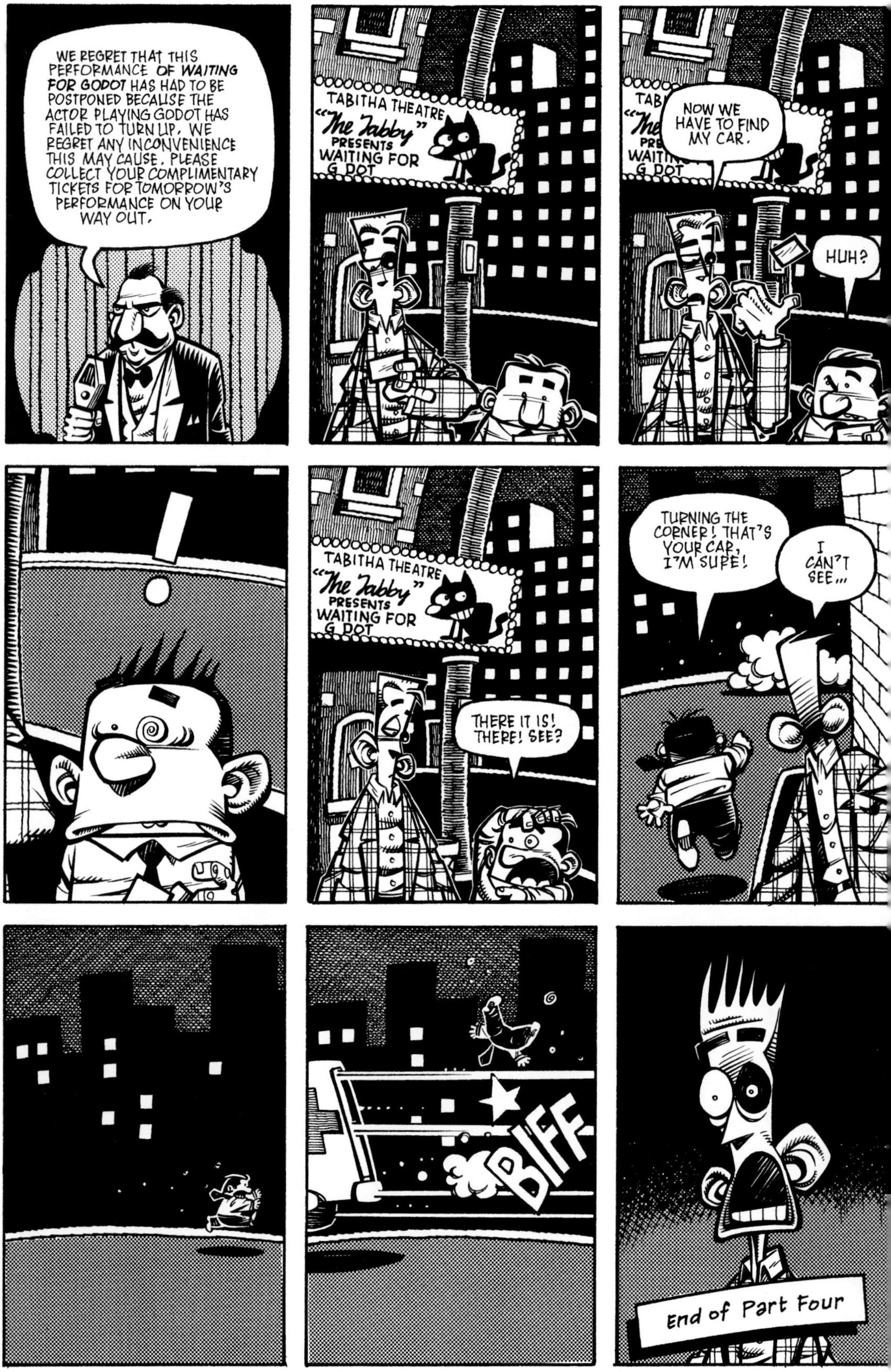
WE REGRET THAT THIS PERFORMANCE OF WAITING FOR GODOT HAS HAD TO BE POSTPONED BECAUSE THE ACTOR PLAYING GODOT HAS FAILED TO TURN UP. WE REGRET ANY INCONVENIENCE THIS MAY CAUSE. PLEASE COLLECT YOUR COMPLIMENTARY TICKETS FOR TOMORROW'S PERFORMANCE ON YOUR WAY OUT.
TABITHA THEATRE "The Tabby" PRESENTS WAITING FOR G DOT
NOW WE HAVE TO FIND MY CAR.
HUH?
TABITHA THEATRE "The Tabby" PRESENTS WAITING FOR G DOT
THERE IT IS! THERE! SEE?
TURNING THE CORNER! THAT'S YOUR CAR, I'M SURE!
I CAN'T SEE...
BIFF
End of Part Four

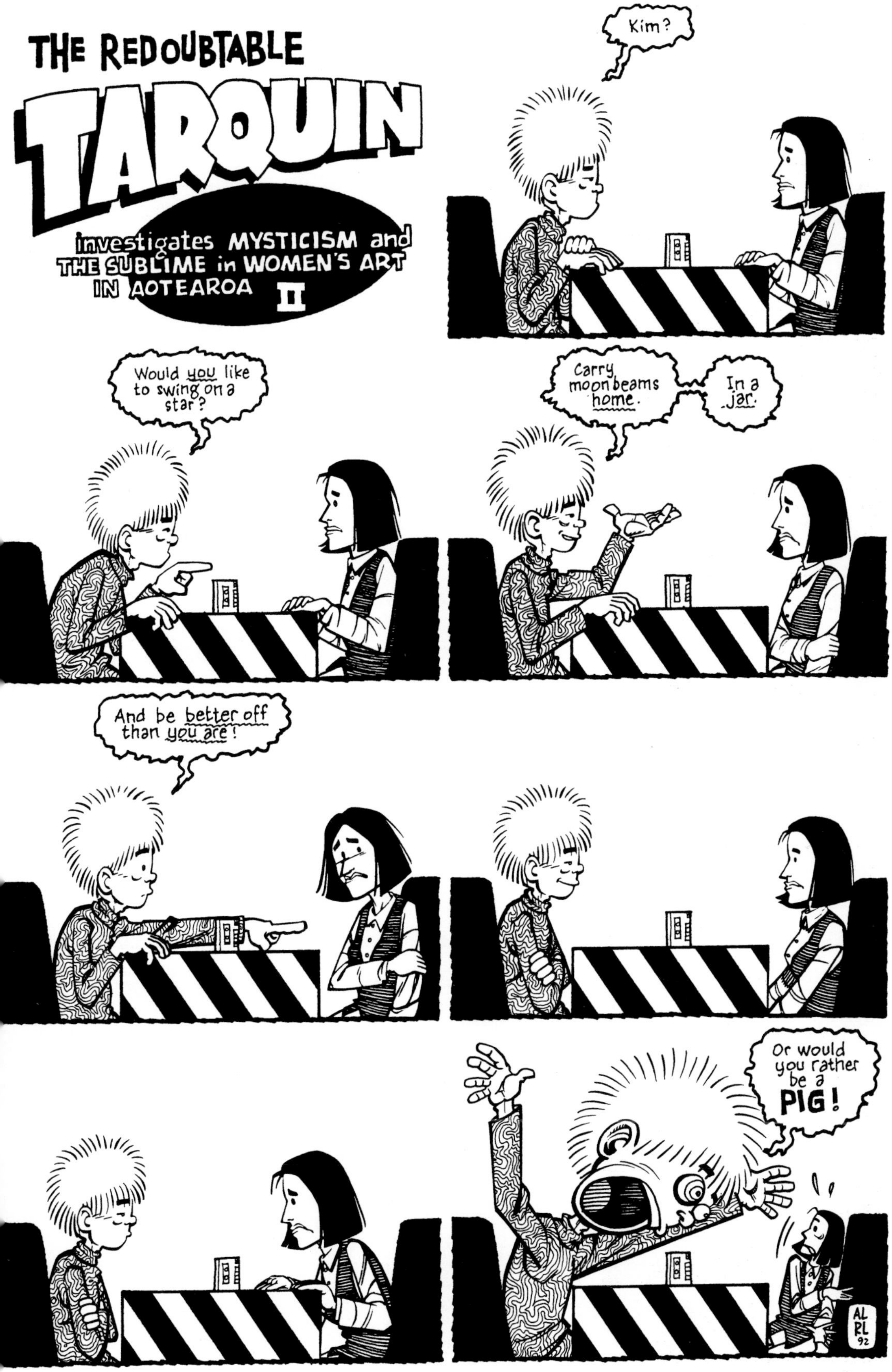
THE REDOUBTABLE
TARQUIN
investigates MYSTICISM and THE SUBLIME in WOMEN'S ART IN AOTEAROA II
Kim?
Would you like to swing on a star?
Carry moonbeams home.
In a jar.
And be better off than you are!
Or would you rather be a PIG!
AL RL 92

THE EGG and SPOON RACE

~ STRIPS FOR THE LAZY CARTOONIST # 43

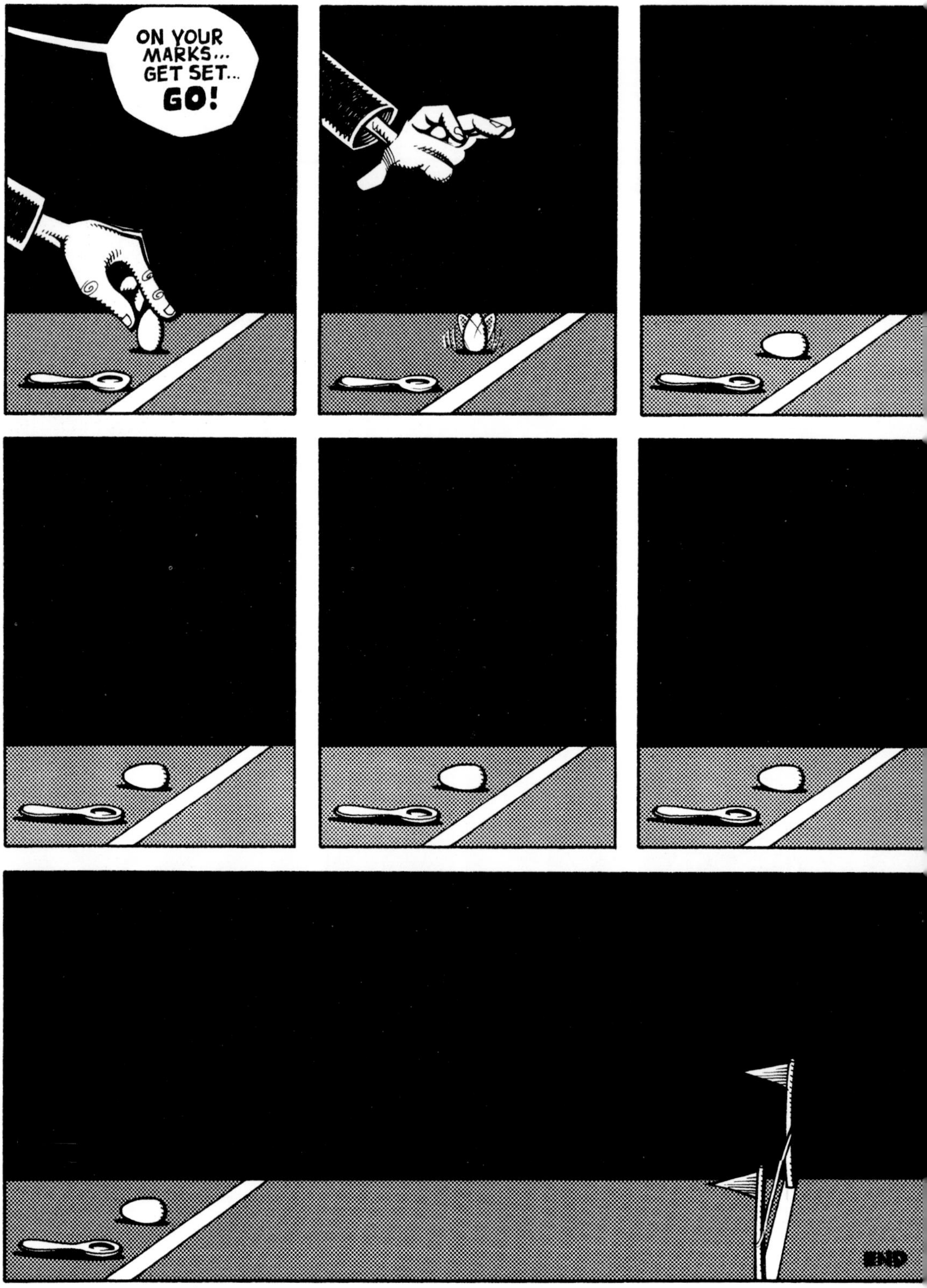
ON YOUR MARKS... GET SET... GO!
END

PREPARE THE ANAESTHETIC.

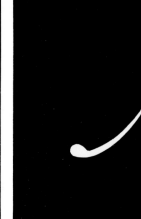

IT'S LUCKY FOR HIM THAT AMBULANCE WAS THERE.

IS THIS HEAVEN OR HELL?

Nixt, neither, nunnabove ...

Obscerve afear y'selve these indentical octuppets ex matre, the Everymam.

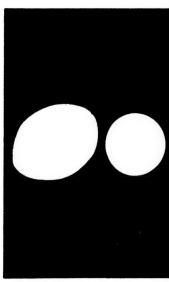

Dainty Al, virgilant commedian

Yeasty Bill, the wee battler, too sure conversioning monget hisselfc retatetatetatet. Conversioning us. List, speak hisstory, usstory.

A split personality these, spourting philosofossicalese, yet a jocastular dorable man: Bigfoot of Athienna.

Monsieur de l'Orange, mush admadred in the chitterly chat of the upper crush.

Ah, Poor Tom o'Bucket, full of watts and wise and woes.

Jokamo Deedledum, preemanent textile purvericator and in deed yours truly.

Buggar off, Tom Agin, the game is upended.

AND ENFINALLY OLD SHAKEBAG, PATER OF EVERONE OF THE ABSENTMINDED BEGGARS USED TO BE SEEM ALUBOUT D'ESE PARSTS.

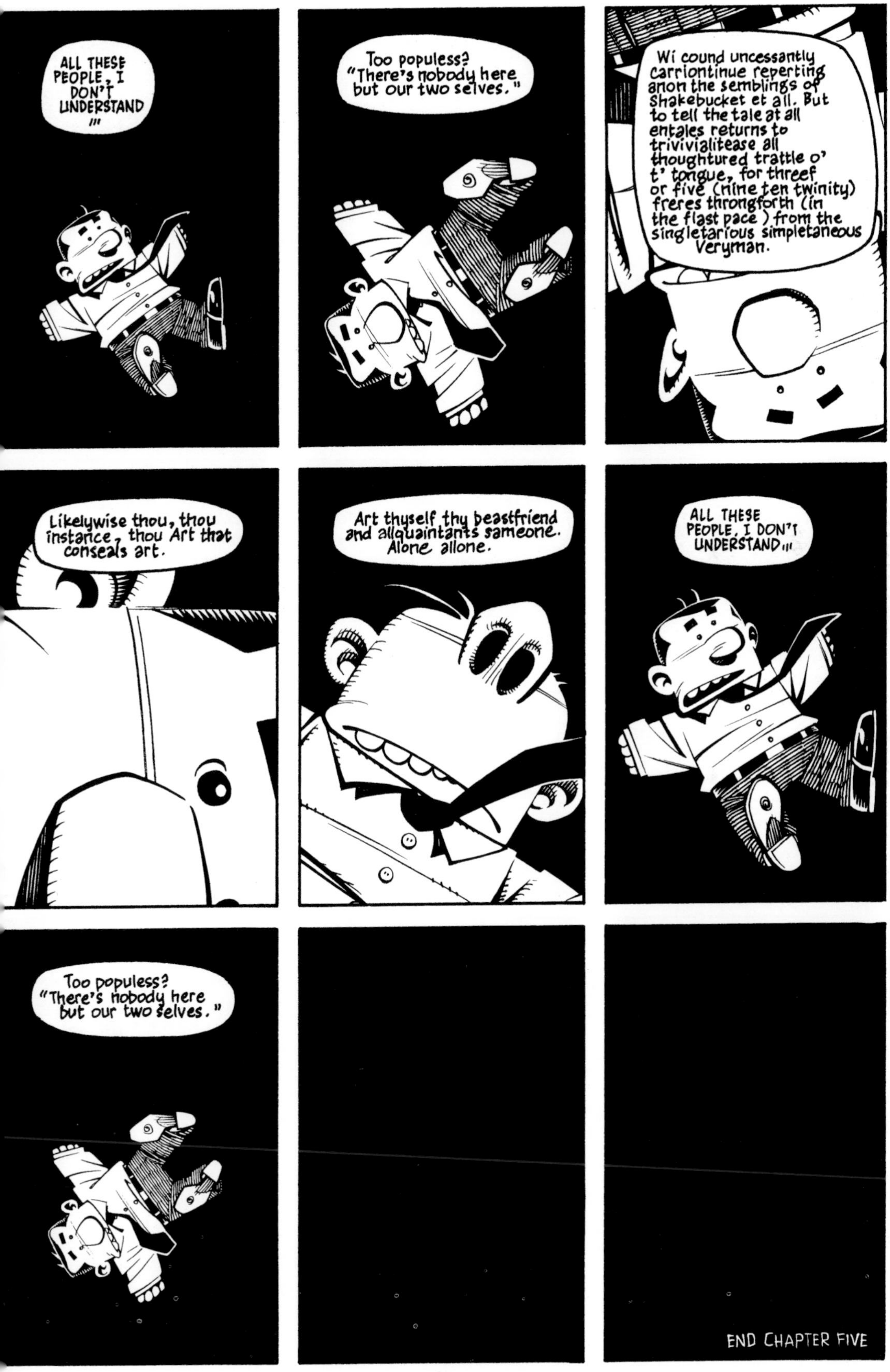

ALL THESE PEOPLE, I DON'T UNDERSTAND ...
Too populess? "There's nobody here but our two selves."
Wi cound uncessantly carriontinue reperting anon the semblings of Shakebucket et all. But to tell the tale at all entales returns to trivivialitease all thoughtured trattle o' t' tongue, for threef or five (nine ten twinity) freres throngforth (in the flast pace) from the singletarious simpletaneous Veryman.
Likelywise thou, thou instance, thou Art that conseals art.
Art thyself thy beastfriend and allquaintants someone. Alone allone.
ALL THESE PEOPLE, I DON'T UNDERSTAND ...
Too populess? "There's nobody here but our two selves."
END CHAPTER FIVE

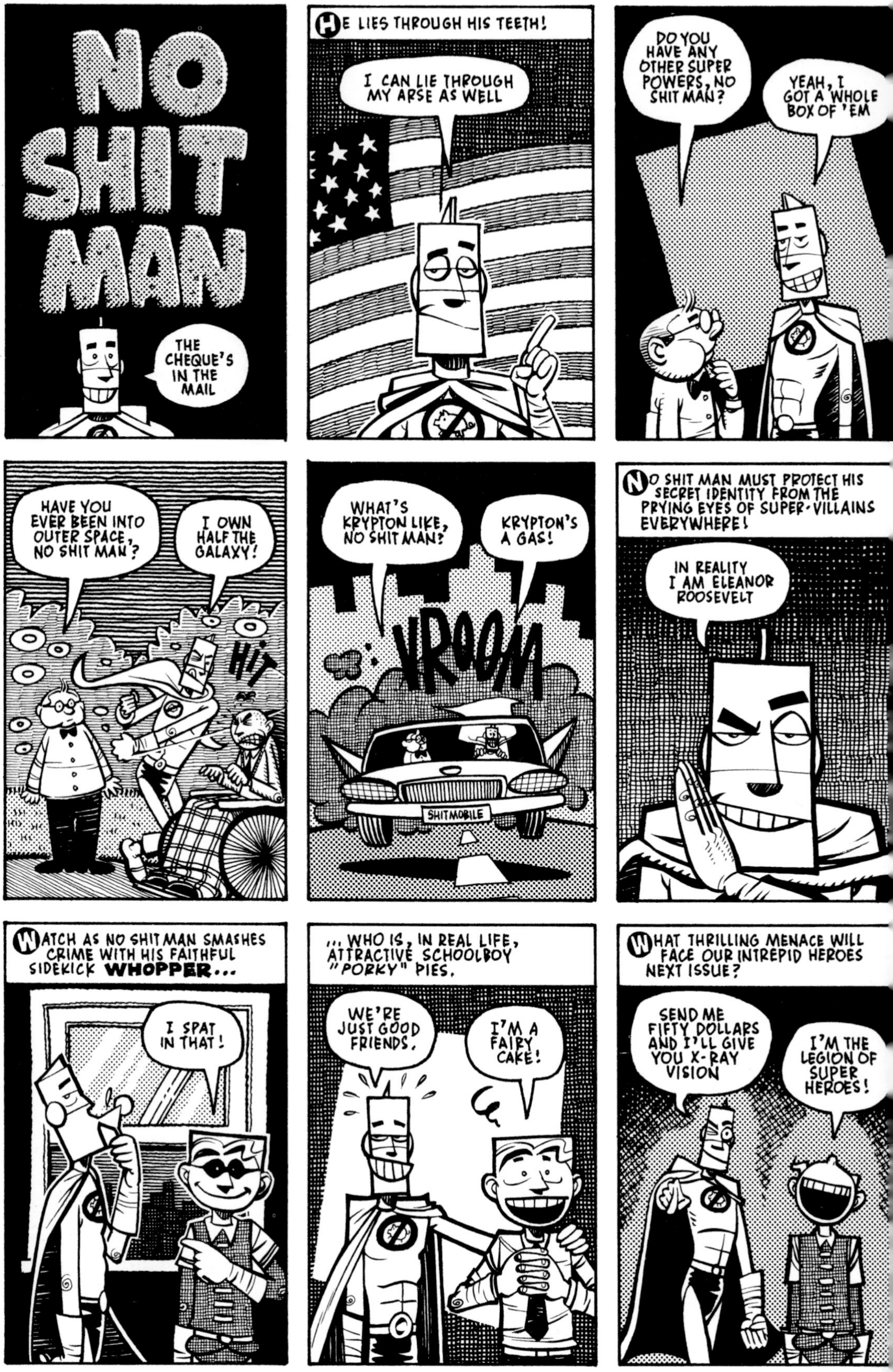
NO SHIT MAN
THE CHEQUE'S IN THE MAIL
HE LIES THROUGH HIS TEETH!
I CAN LIE THROUGH MY ARSE AS WELL
DO YOU HAVE ANY OTHER SUPER POWERS, NO SHIT MAN?
YEAH, I GOT A WHOLE BOX OF 'EM
HAVE YOU EVER BEEN INTO OUTER SPACE, NO SHIT MAN?
I OWN HALF THE GALAXY!
HIT
WHAT'S KRYPTON LIKE, NO SHIT MAN?
KRYPTON'S A GAS!
VROOM
SHITMOBILE
NO SHIT MAN MUST PROTECT HIS SECRET IDENTITY FROM THE PRYING EYES OF SUPER-VILLAINS EVERYWHERE!
IN REALITY I AM ELEANOR ROOSEVELT
WATCH AS NO SHIT MAN SMASHES CRIME WITH HIS FAITHFUL SIDEKICK WHOPPER...
I SPAT IN THAT!
... WHO IS, IN REAL LIFE, ATTRACTIVE SCHOOLBOY "PORKY" PIES.
WE'RE JUST GOOD FRIENDS.
I'M A FAIRY CAKE!
WHAT THRILLING MENACE WILL FACE OUR INTREPID HEROES NEXT ISSUE?
SEND ME FIFTY DOLLARS AND I'LL GIVE YOU X-RAY VISION
I'M THE LEGION OF SUPER HEROES!

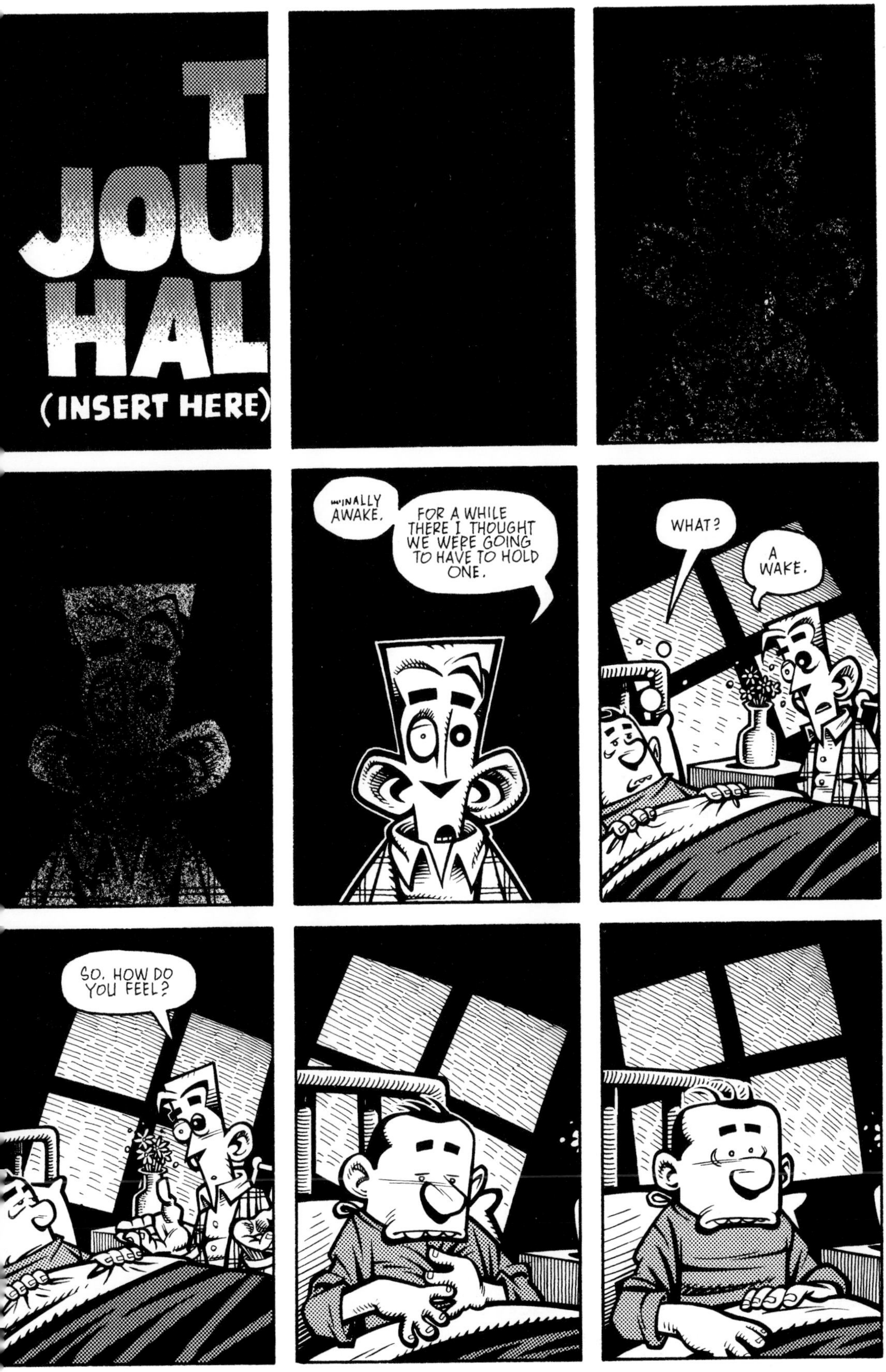
T
JOU
HAL
(INSERT HERE)
...INALLY AWAKE.
FOR A WHILE THERE I THOUGHT WE WERE GOING TO HAVE TO HOLD ONE.
WHAT?
A WAKE.
SO, HOW DO YOU FEEL?

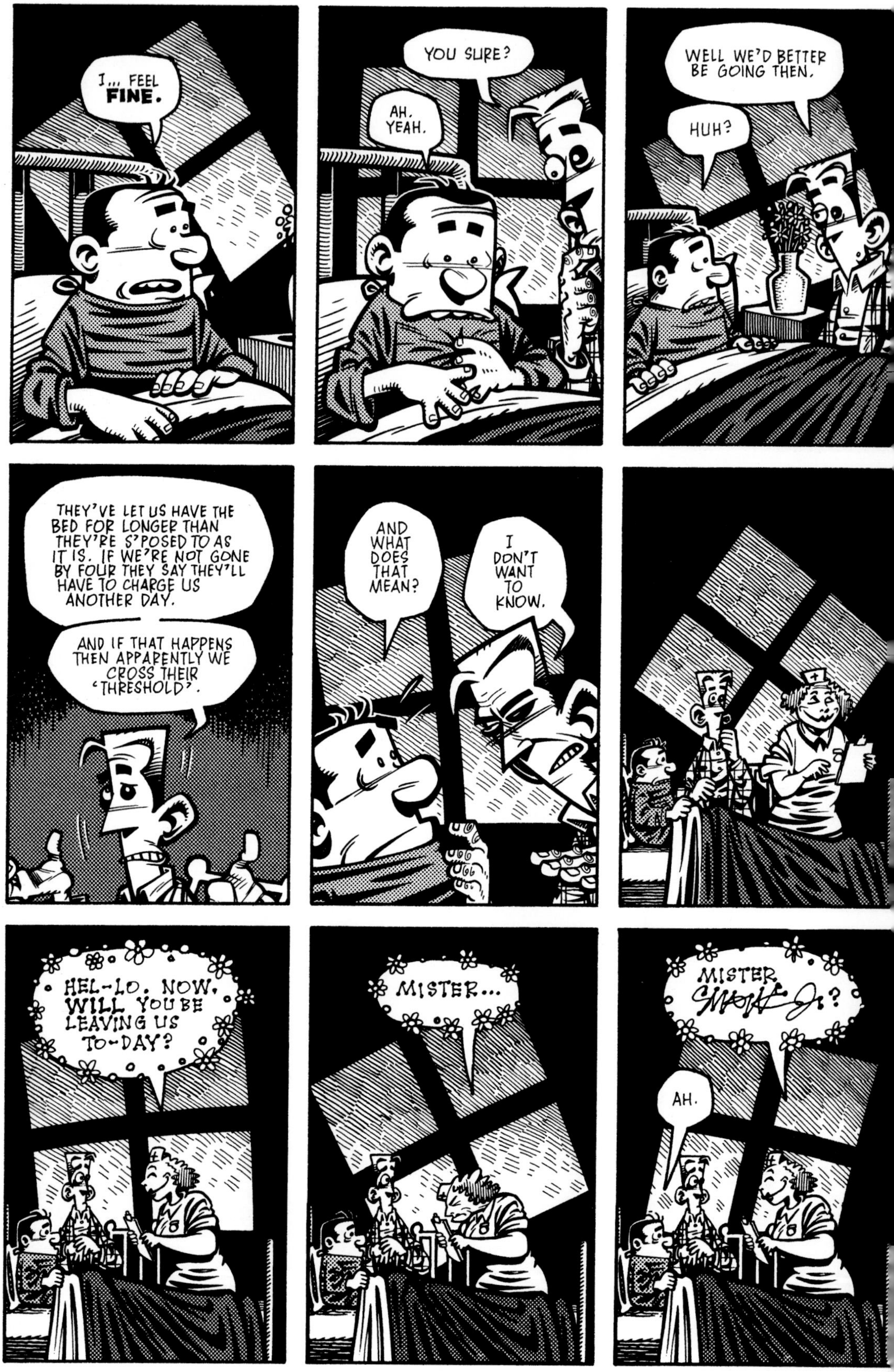
I... FEEL FINE.
YOU SURE?
AH, YEAH.
WELL WE'D BETTER BE GOING THEN.
HUH?
THEY'VE LET US HAVE THE BED FOR LONGER THAN THEY'RE S'POSED TO AS IT IS. IF WE'RE NOT GONE BY FOUR THEY SAY THEY'LL HAVE TO CHARGE US ANOTHER DAY.
AND IF THAT HAPPENS THEN APPARENTLY WE CROSS THEIR 'THRESHOLD'.
AND WHAT DOES THAT MEAN?
I DON'T WANT TO KNOW.
HEL-LO. NOW, WILL YOU BE LEAVING US TO-DAY?
MISTER...
MISTER ?
AH.

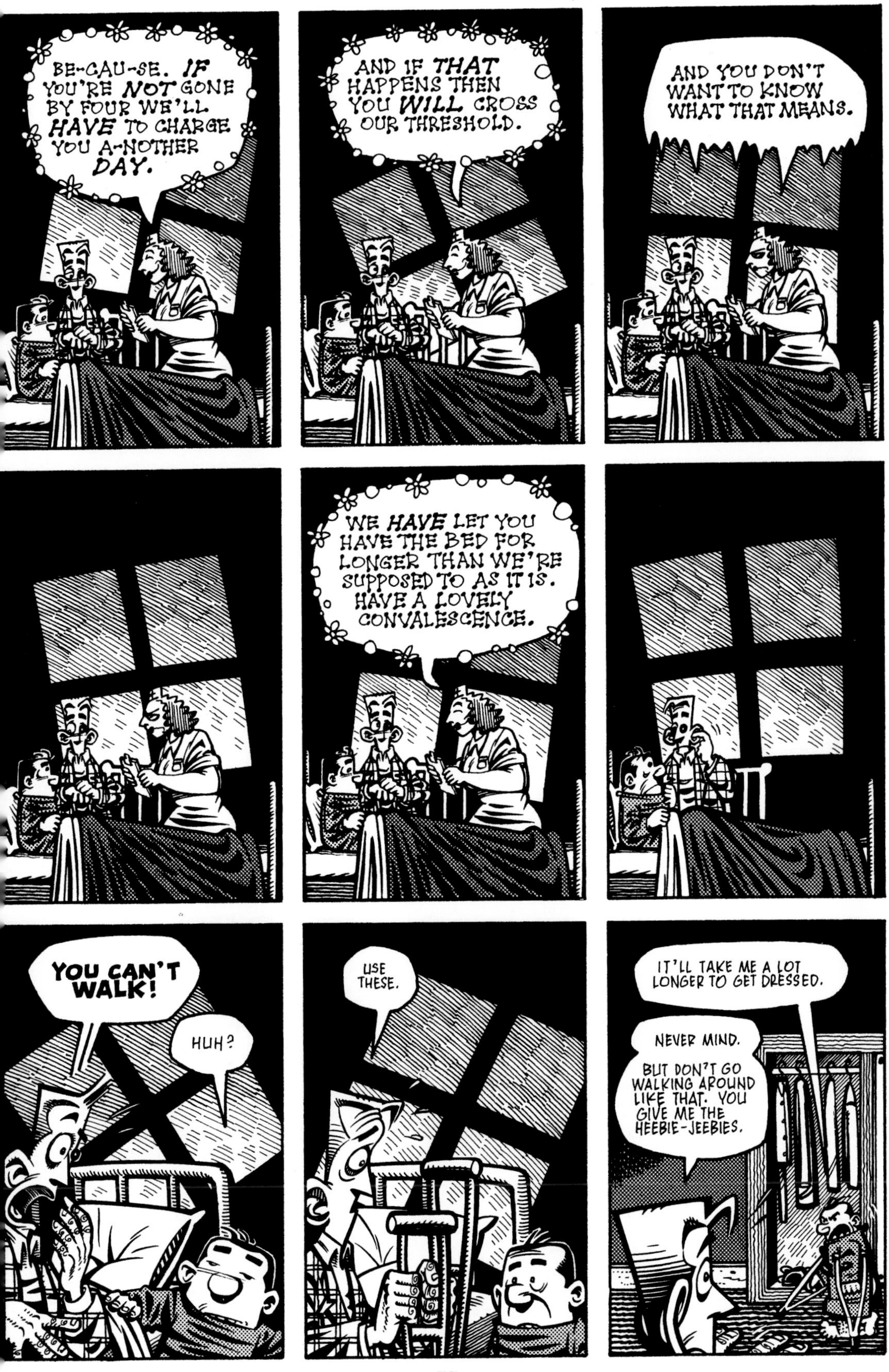

BE-CAU-SE. IF YOU'RE NOT GONE BY FOUR WE'LL HAVE TO CHARGE YOU A-NOTHER DAY.
AND IF THAT HAPPENS THEN YOU WILL CROSS OUR THRESHOLD.
AND YOU DON'T WANT TO KNOW WHAT THAT MEANS.
WE HAVE LET YOU HAVE THE BED FOR LONGER THAN WE'RE SUPPOSED TO AS IT IS. HAVE A LOVELY CONVALESCENCE.
YOU CAN'T WALK!
HUH?
USE THESE.
IT'LL TAKE ME A LOT LONGER TO GET DRESSED.
NEVER MIND.
BUT DON'T GO WALKING AROUND LIKE THAT. YOU GIVE ME THE HEEBIE-JEEBIES.

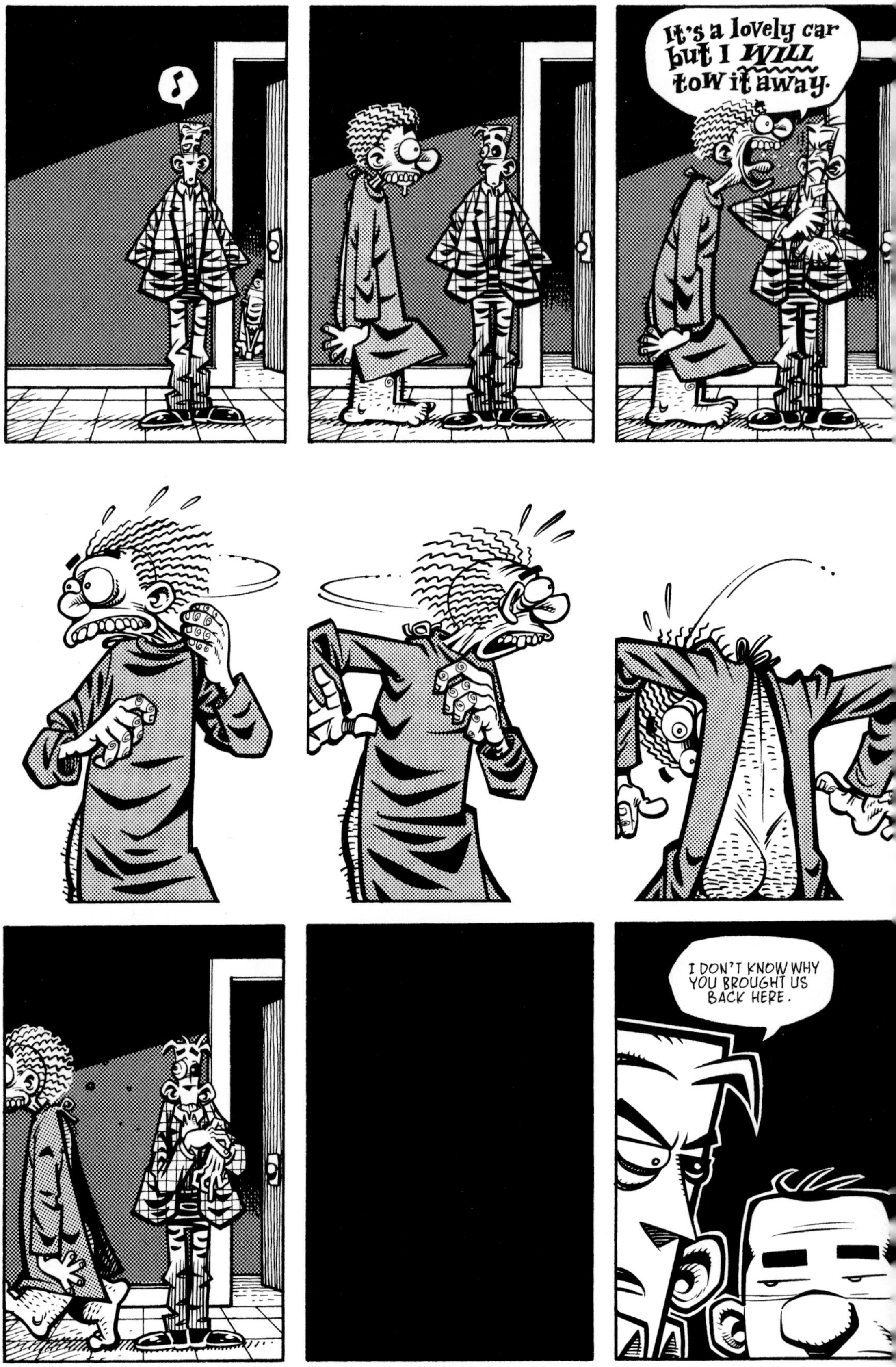
It's a lovely car but I WILL tow it away.
I DON'T KNOW WHY YOU BROUGHT US BACK HERE.

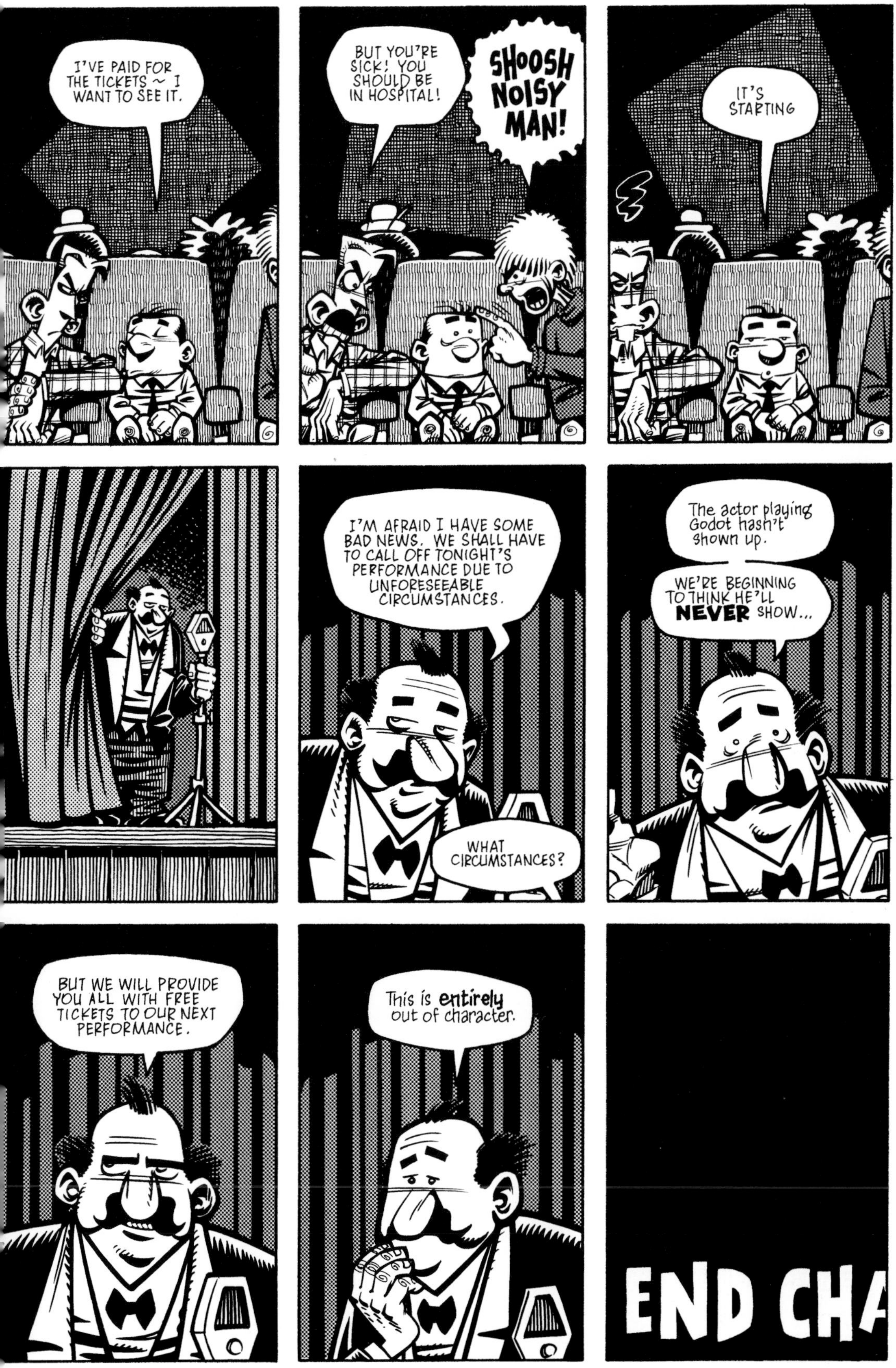
I'VE PAID FOR THE TICKETS ~ I WANT TO SEE IT.
BUT YOU'RE SICK! YOU SHOULD BE IN HOSPITAL!
SHOOSH NOISY MAN!
IT'S STARTING
I'M AFRAID I HAVE SOME BAD NEWS. WE SHALL HAVE TO CALL OFF TONIGHT'S PERFORMANCE DUE TO UNFORESEEABLE CIRCUMSTANCES.
WHAT CIRCUMSTANCES?
The actor playing Godot hasn't shown up.
WE'RE BEGINNING TO THINK HE'LL NEVER SHOW...
BUT WE WILL PROVIDE YOU ALL WITH FREE TICKETS TO OUR NEXT PERFORMANCE.
This is entirely out of character.
END CHA

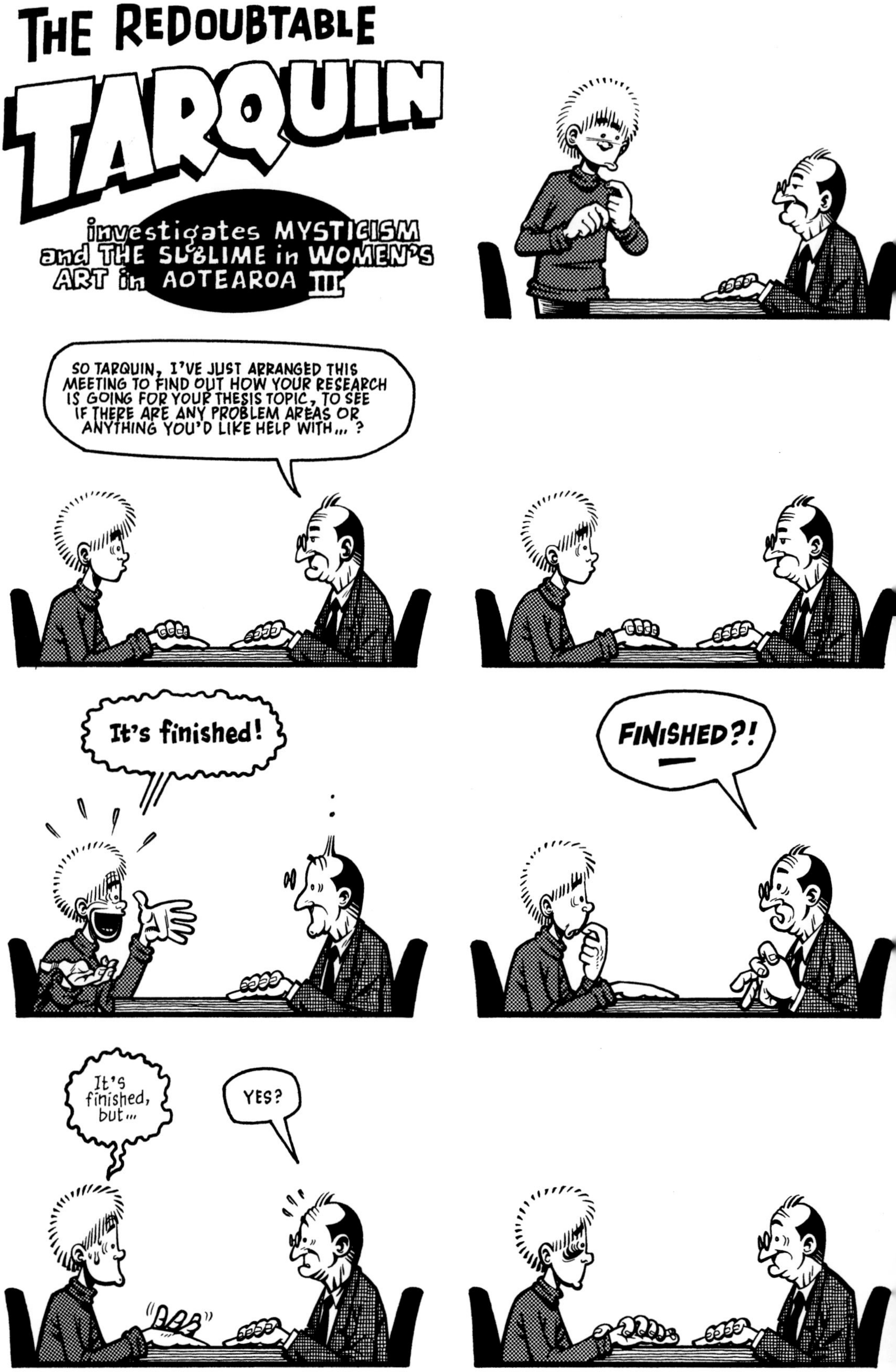
THE REDOUBTABLE
TARQUIN
investigates MYSTICISM and THE SUBLIME in WOMEN'S ART in AOTEAROA III
SO TARQUIN, I'VE JUST ARRANGED THIS MEETING TO FIND OUT HOW YOUR RESEARCH IS GOING FOR YOUR THESIS TOPIC, TO SEE IF THERE ARE ANY PROBLEM AREAS OR ANYTHING YOU'D LIKE HELP WITH... ?
It's finished!
FINISHED?!
It's finished, but...
YES?

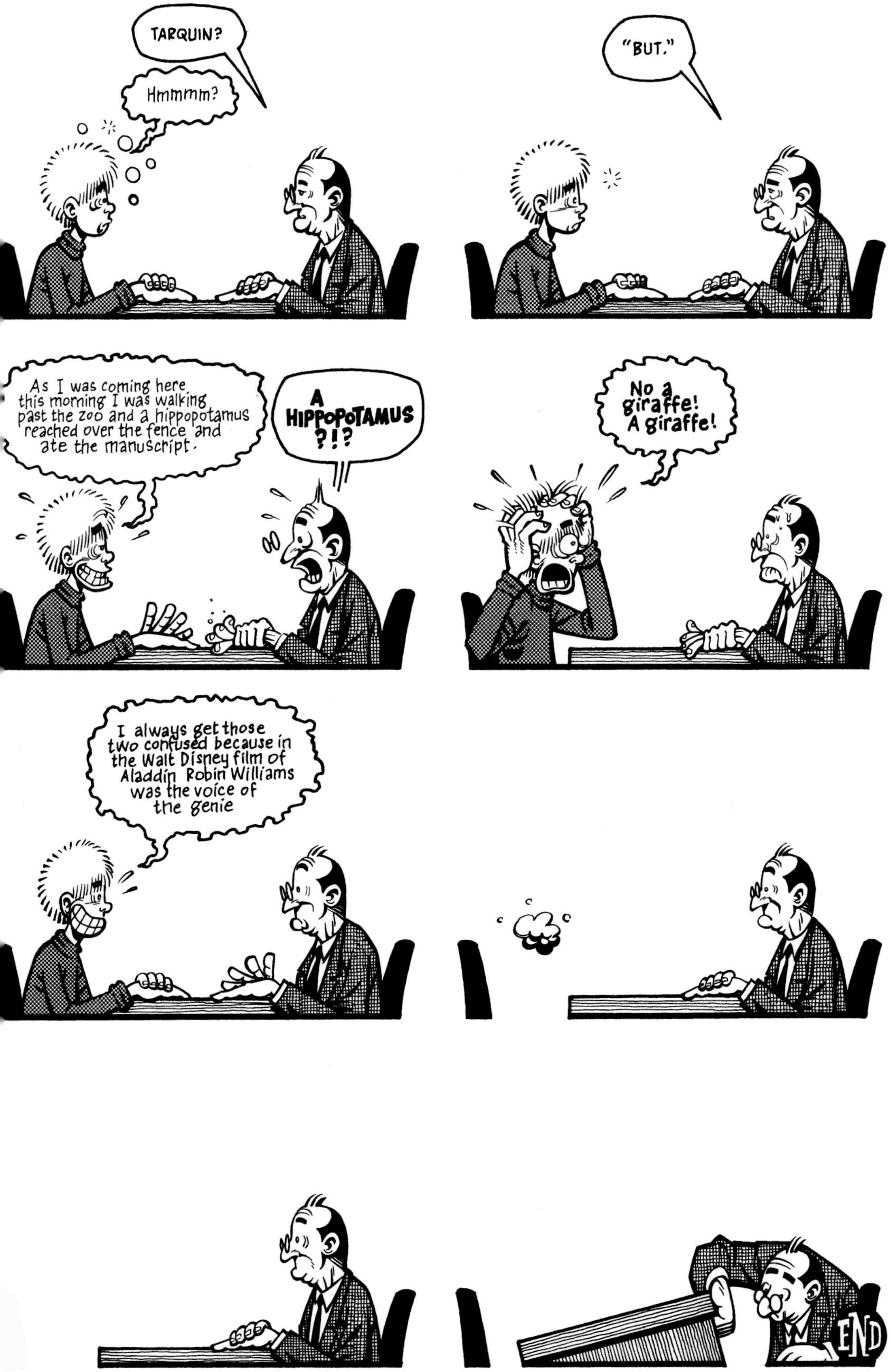
TARQUIN?
Hmmmm?
"BUT."
As I was coming here this morning I was walking past the zoo and a hippopotamus reached over the fence and ate the manuscript.
A HIPPOPOTAMUS ?!?
No a giraffe! A giraffe!
I always get those two confused because in the Walt Disney film of Aladdin Robin Williams was the voice of the genie
END

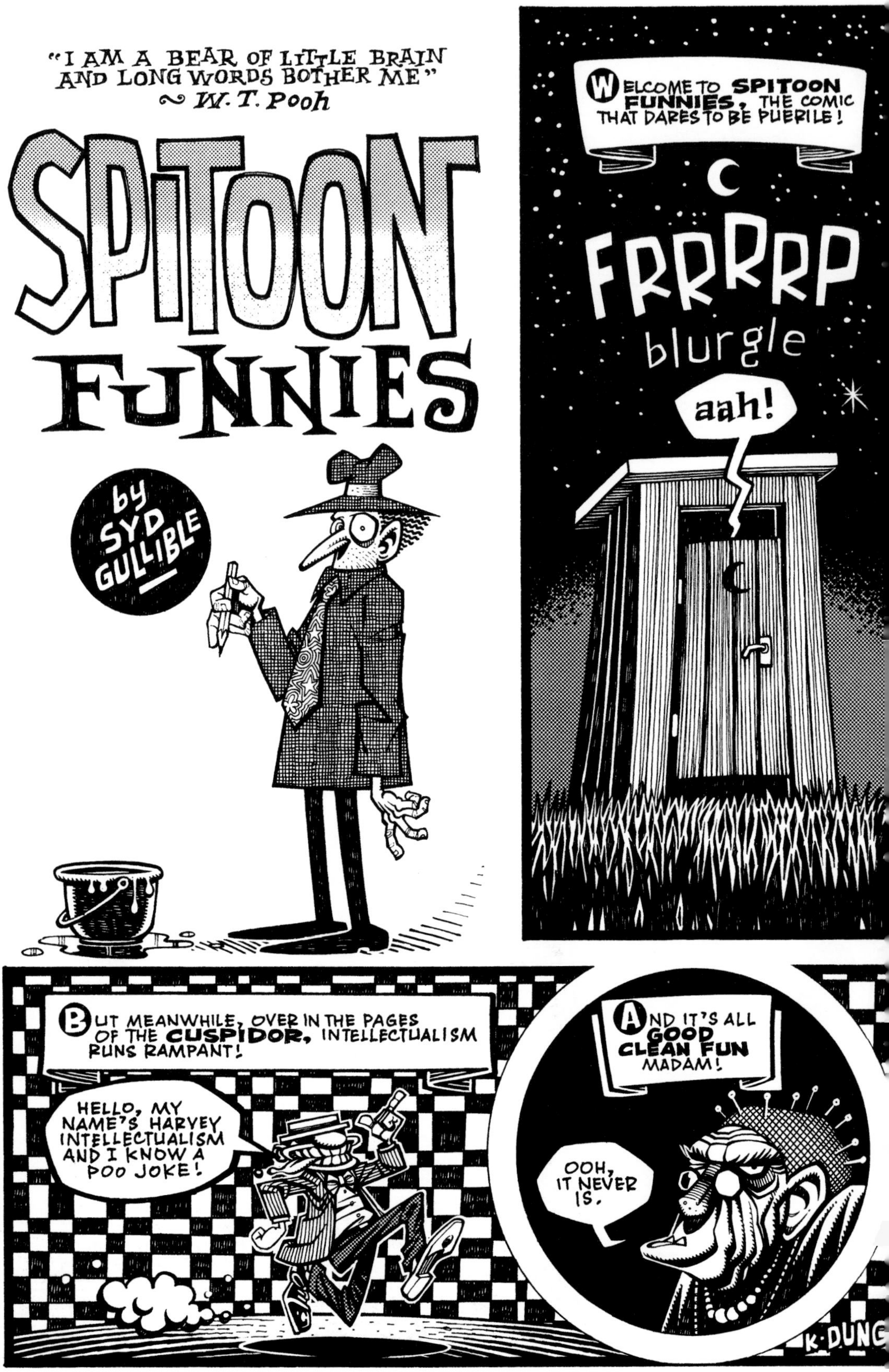
"I AM A BEAR OF LITTLE BRAIN AND LONG WORDS BOTHER ME"
~ W. T. Pooh
SPITOON FUNNIES
by SYD GULLIBLE
WELCOME TO SPITOON FUNNIES, THE COMIC THAT DARES TO BE PUERILE!
FRRRRP
blurgle
aah!
BUT MEANWHILE, OVER IN THE PAGES OF THE CUSPIDOR, INTELLECTUALISM RUNS RAMPANT!
HELLO, MY NAME'S HARVEY INTELLECTUALISM AND I KNOW A POO JOKE!
AND IT'S ALL GOOD CLEAN FUN MADAM!
OOH, IT NEVER IS.
K-DUNC

La Journée Parfaite

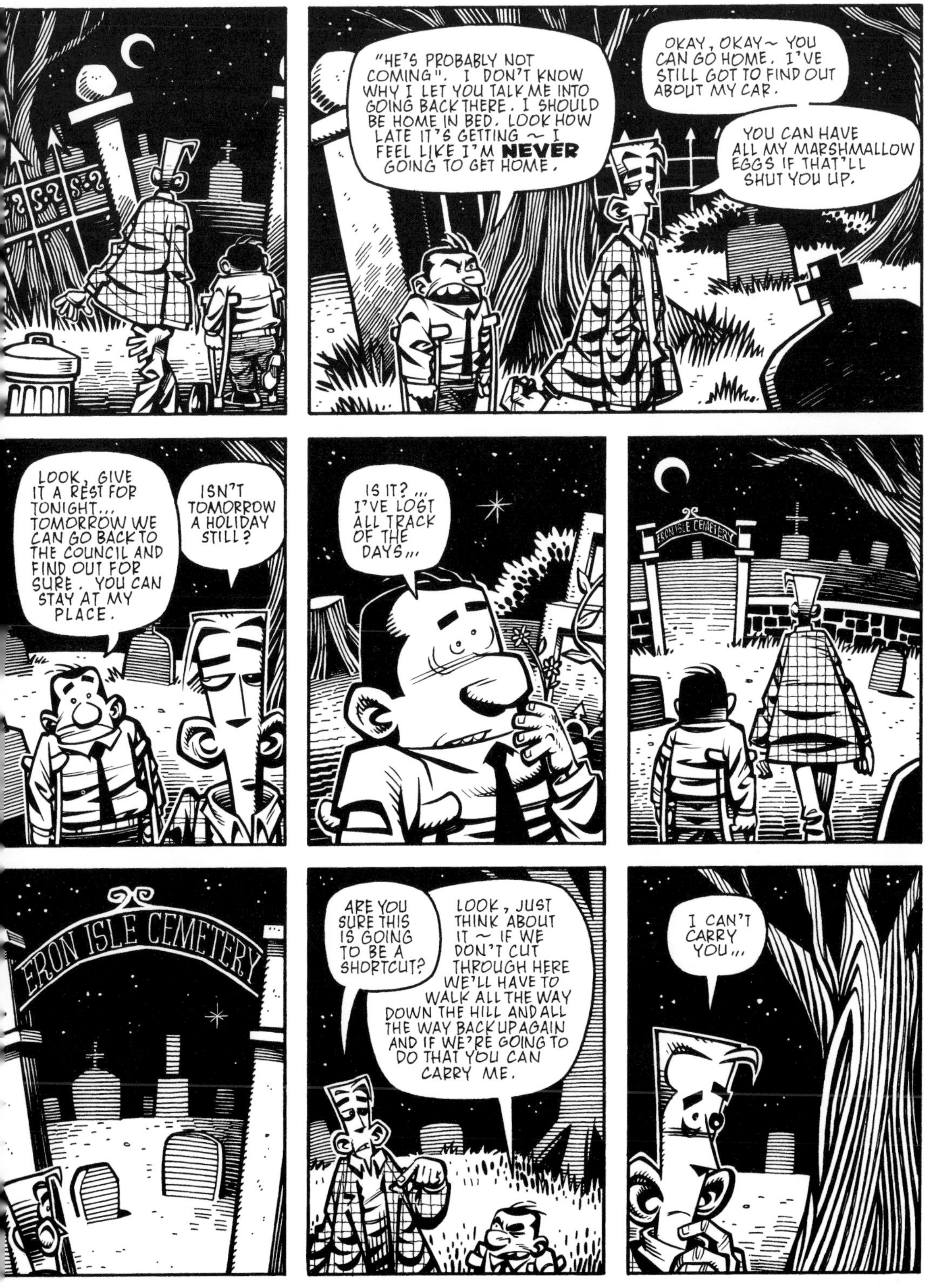

"HE'S PROBABLY NOT COMING". I DON'T KNOW WHY I LET YOU TALK ME INTO GOING BACK THERE. I SHOULD BE HOME IN BED. LOOK HOW LATE IT'S GETTING ~ I FEEL LIKE I'M **NEVER** GOING TO GET HOME.
OKAY, OKAY ~ YOU CAN GO HOME. I'VE STILL GOT TO FIND OUT ABOUT MY CAR.
YOU CAN HAVE ALL MY MARSHMALLOW EGGS IF THAT'LL SHUT YOU UP.
LOOK, GIVE IT A REST FOR TONIGHT... TOMORROW WE CAN GO BACK TO THE COUNCIL AND FIND OUT FOR SURE. YOU CAN STAY AT MY PLACE.
ISN'T TOMORROW A HOLIDAY STILL?
IS IT? ... I'VE LOST ALL TRACK OF THE DAYS...
ERON ISLE CEMETERY
ERON ISLE CEMETERY
ARE YOU SURE THIS IS GOING TO BE A SHORTCUT?
LOOK, JUST THINK ABOUT IT ~ IF WE DON'T CUT THROUGH HERE WE'LL HAVE TO WALK ALL THE WAY DOWN THE HILL AND ALL THE WAY BACK UP AGAIN AND IF WE'RE GOING TO DO THAT YOU CAN CARRY ME.
I CAN'T CARRY YOU...

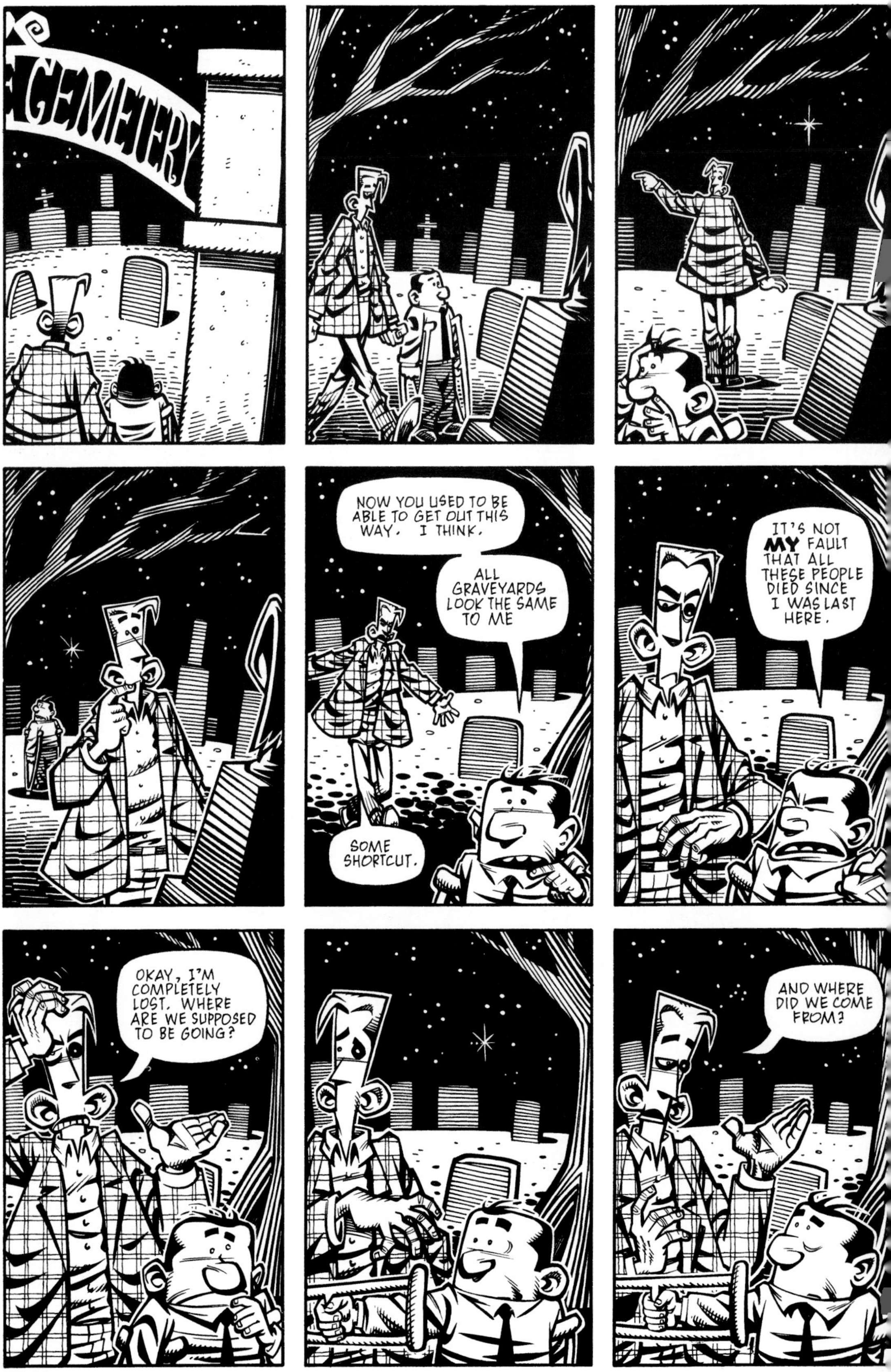
CEMETERY
NOW YOU USED TO BE ABLE TO GET OUT THIS WAY. I THINK.
ALL GRAVEYARDS LOOK THE SAME TO ME
SOME SHORTCUT.
IT'S NOT **MY** FAULT THAT ALL THESE PEOPLE DIED SINCE I WAS LAST HERE.
OKAY, I'M COMPLETELY LOST. WHERE ARE WE SUPPOSED TO BE GOING?
AND WHERE DID WE COME FROM?

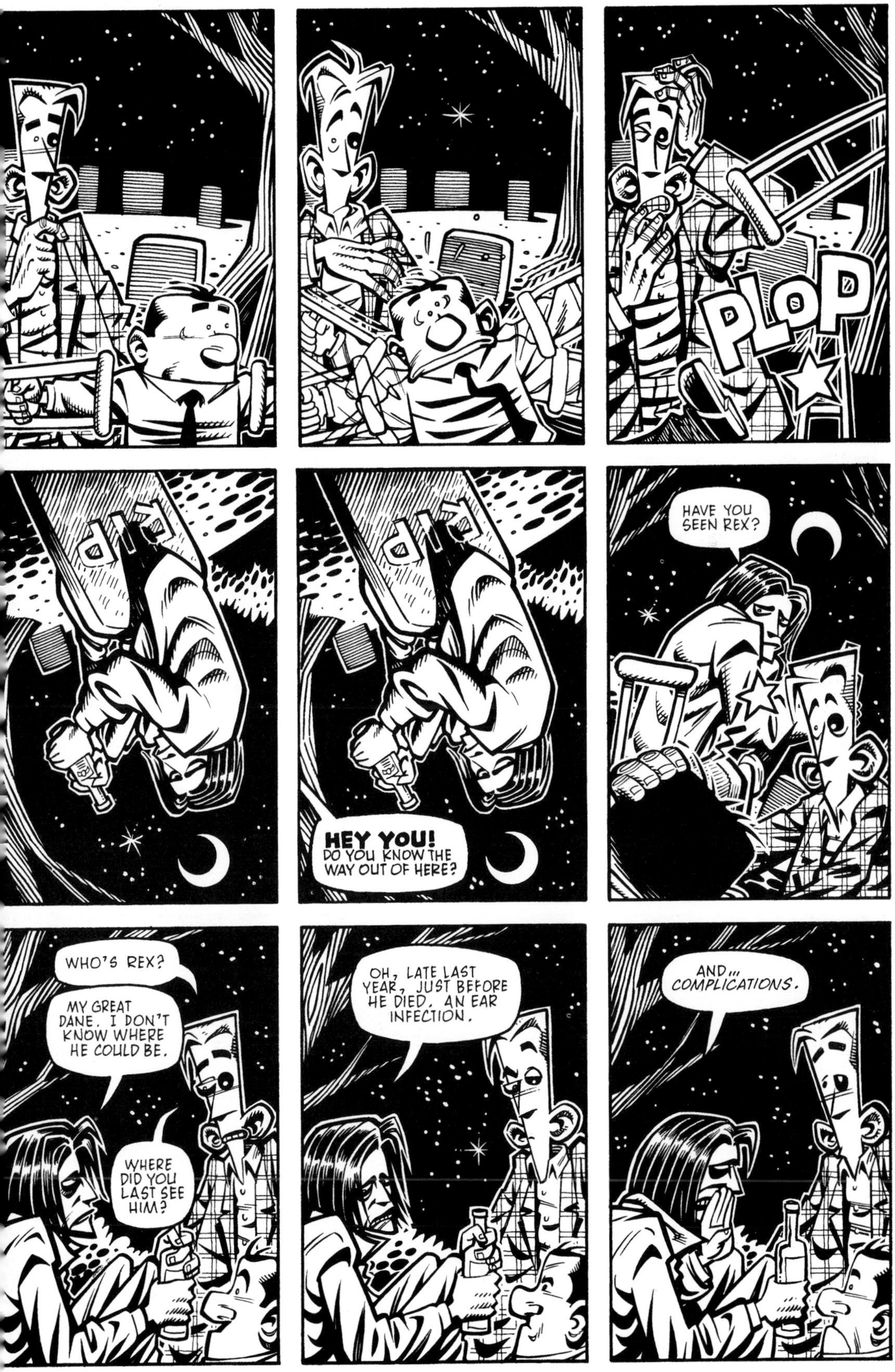
PLOP
HEY YOU!
DO YOU KNOW THE WAY OUT OF HERE?
HAVE YOU SEEN REX?
WHO'S REX?
MY GREAT DANE. I DON'T KNOW WHERE HE COULD BE.
WHERE DID YOU LAST SEE HIM?
OH, LATE LAST YEAR, JUST BEFORE HE DIED. AN EAR INFECTION.
AND... COMPLICATIONS.

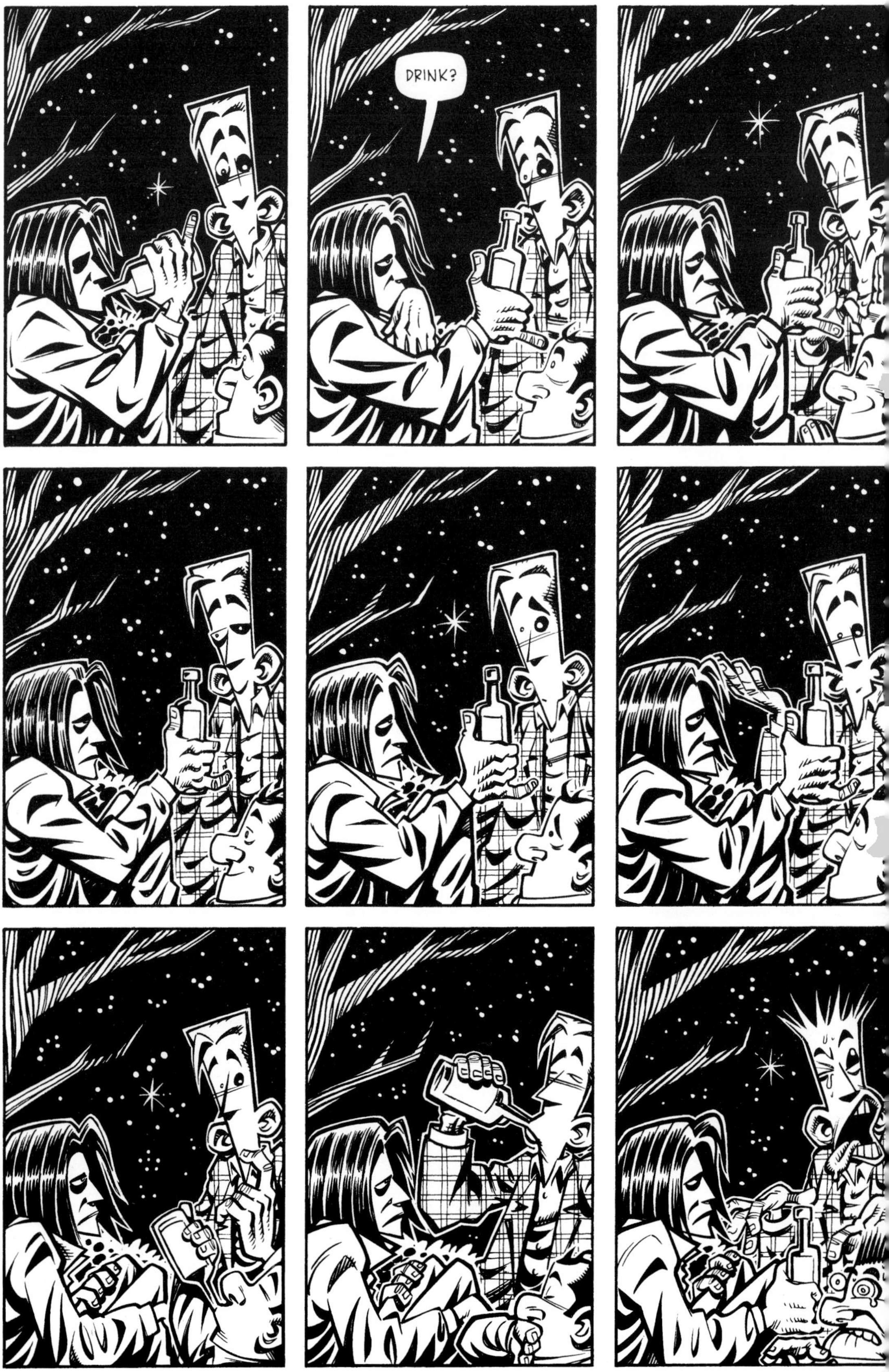
DRINK?

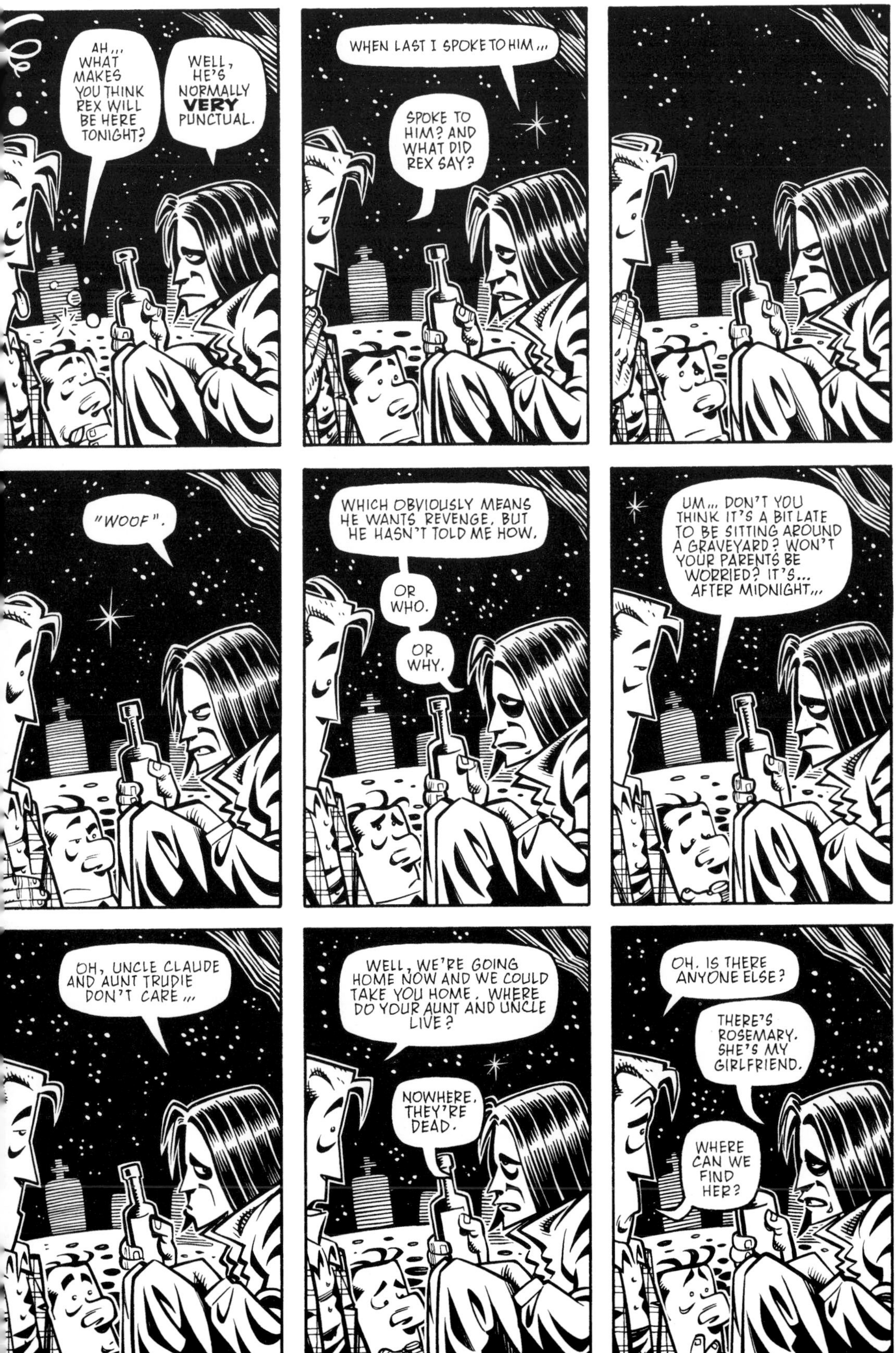
AH... WHAT MAKES YOU THINK REX WILL BE HERE TONIGHT?
WELL, HE'S NORMALLY VERY PUNCTUAL.
WHEN LAST I SPOKE TO HIM...
SPOKE TO HIM? AND WHAT DID REX SAY?
"WOOF".
WHICH OBVIOUSLY MEANS HE WANTS REVENGE, BUT HE HASN'T TOLD ME HOW.
OR WHO.
OR WHY.
UM... DON'T YOU THINK IT'S A BIT LATE TO BE SITTING AROUND A GRAVEYARD? WON'T YOUR PARENTS BE WORRIED? IT'S... AFTER MIDNIGHT...
OH, UNCLE CLAUDE AND AUNT TRUDIE DON'T CARE...
WELL, WE'RE GOING HOME NOW AND WE COULD TAKE YOU HOME. WHERE DO YOUR AUNT AND UNCLE LIVE?
NOWHERE. THEY'RE DEAD.
OH. IS THERE ANYONE ELSE?
THERE'S ROSEMARY. SHE'S MY GIRLFRIEND.
WHERE CAN WE FIND HER?

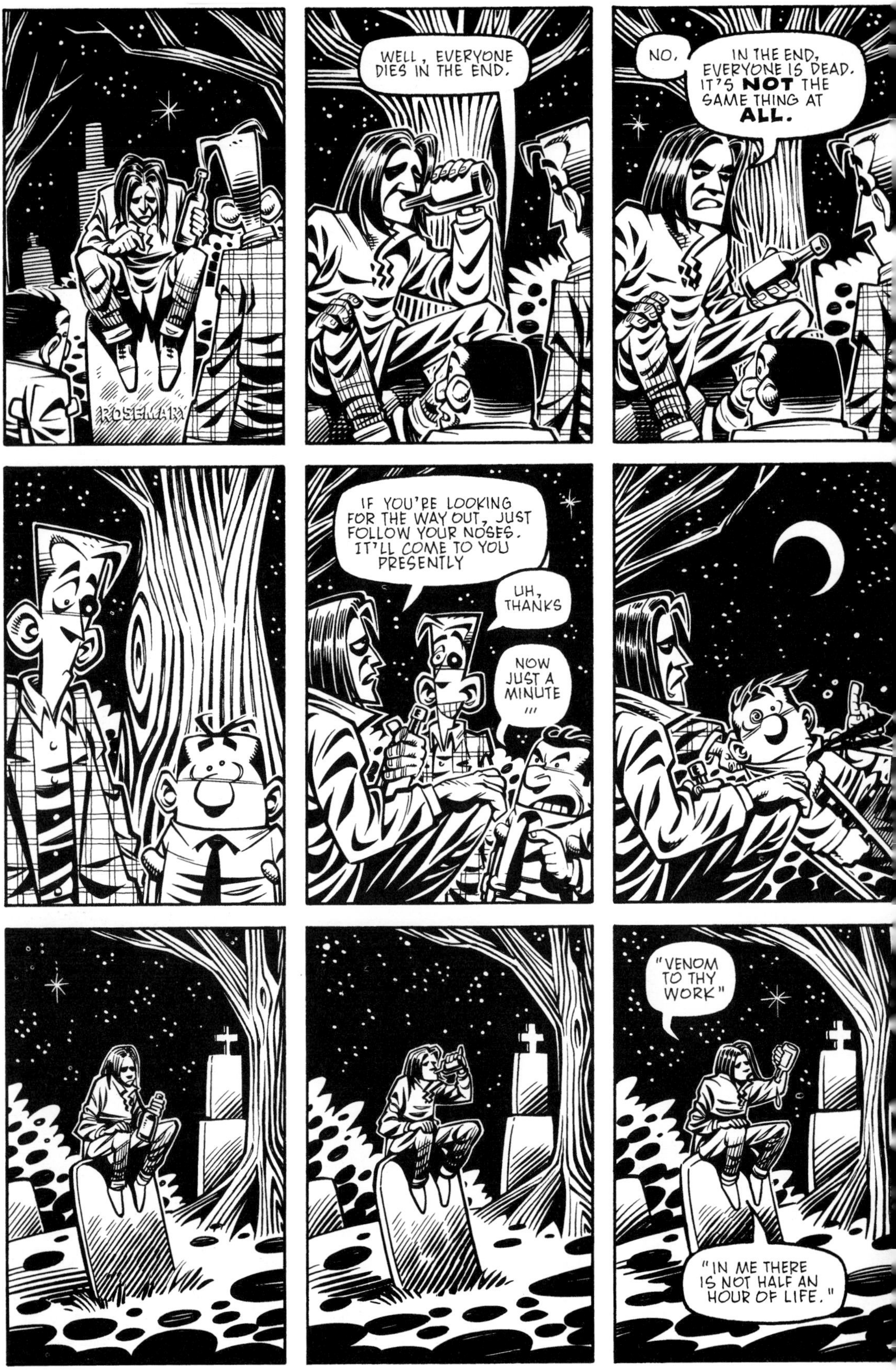
ROSEMARY
WELL, EVERYONE DIES IN THE END.
NO,
IN THE END, EVERYONE IS DEAD. IT'S **NOT** THE SAME THING AT **ALL.**
IF YOU'RE LOOKING FOR THE WAY OUT, JUST FOLLOW YOUR NOSES. IT'LL COME TO YOU PRESENTLY
UH, THANKS
NOW JUST A MINUTE ...
"VENOM TO THY WORK"
"IN ME THERE IS NOT HALF AN HOUR OF LIFE."

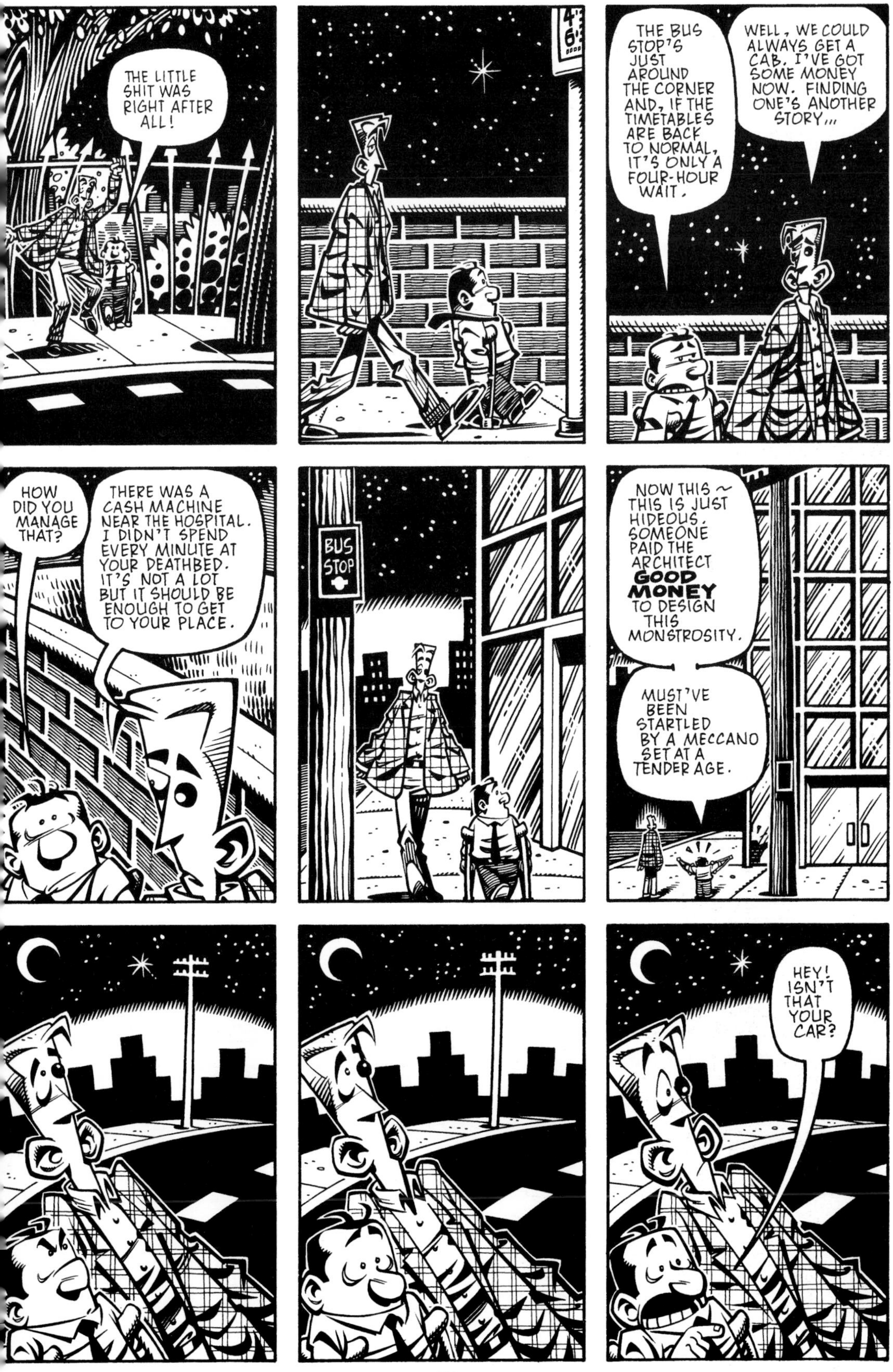
THE LITTLE SHIT WAS RIGHT AFTER ALL!
THE BUS STOP'S JUST AROUND THE CORNER AND, IF THE TIMETABLES ARE BACK TO NORMAL, IT'S ONLY A FOUR-HOUR WAIT.
WELL, WE COULD ALWAYS GET A CAB. I'VE GOT SOME MONEY NOW. FINDING ONE'S ANOTHER STORY...
HOW DID YOU MANAGE THAT?
THERE WAS A CASH MACHINE NEAR THE HOSPITAL. I DIDN'T SPEND EVERY MINUTE AT YOUR DEATHBED. IT'S NOT A LOT BUT IT SHOULD BE ENOUGH TO GET TO YOUR PLACE.
BUS STOP
NOW THIS ~ THIS IS JUST HIDEOUS. SOMEONE PAID THE ARCHITECT GOOD MONEY TO DESIGN THIS MONSTROSITY.
MUST'VE BEEN STARTLED BY A MECCANO SET AT A TENDER AGE.
HEY! ISN'T THAT YOUR CAR?

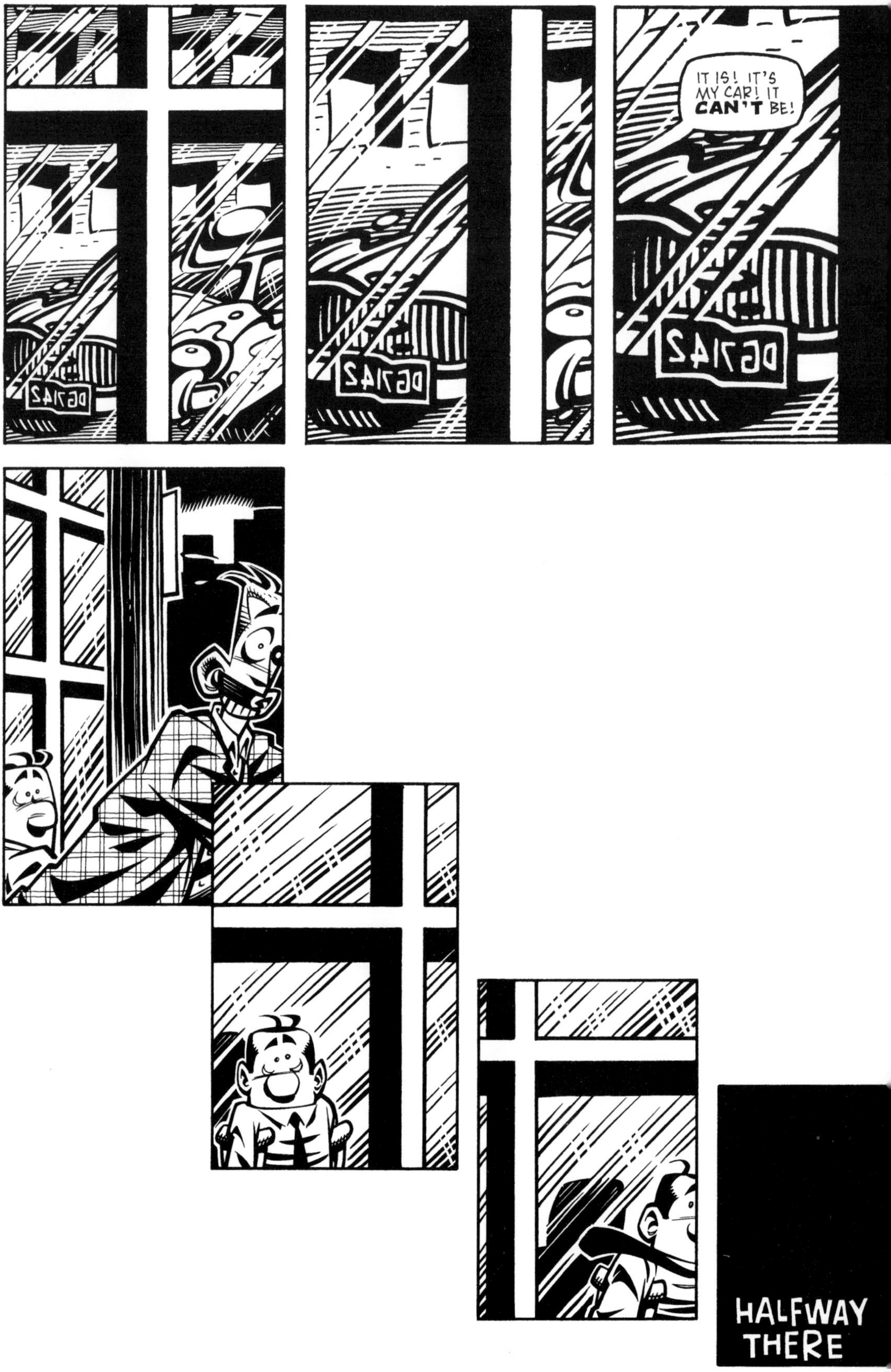
IT IS! IT'S MY CAR! IT **CAN'T** BE!
HALFWAY THERE

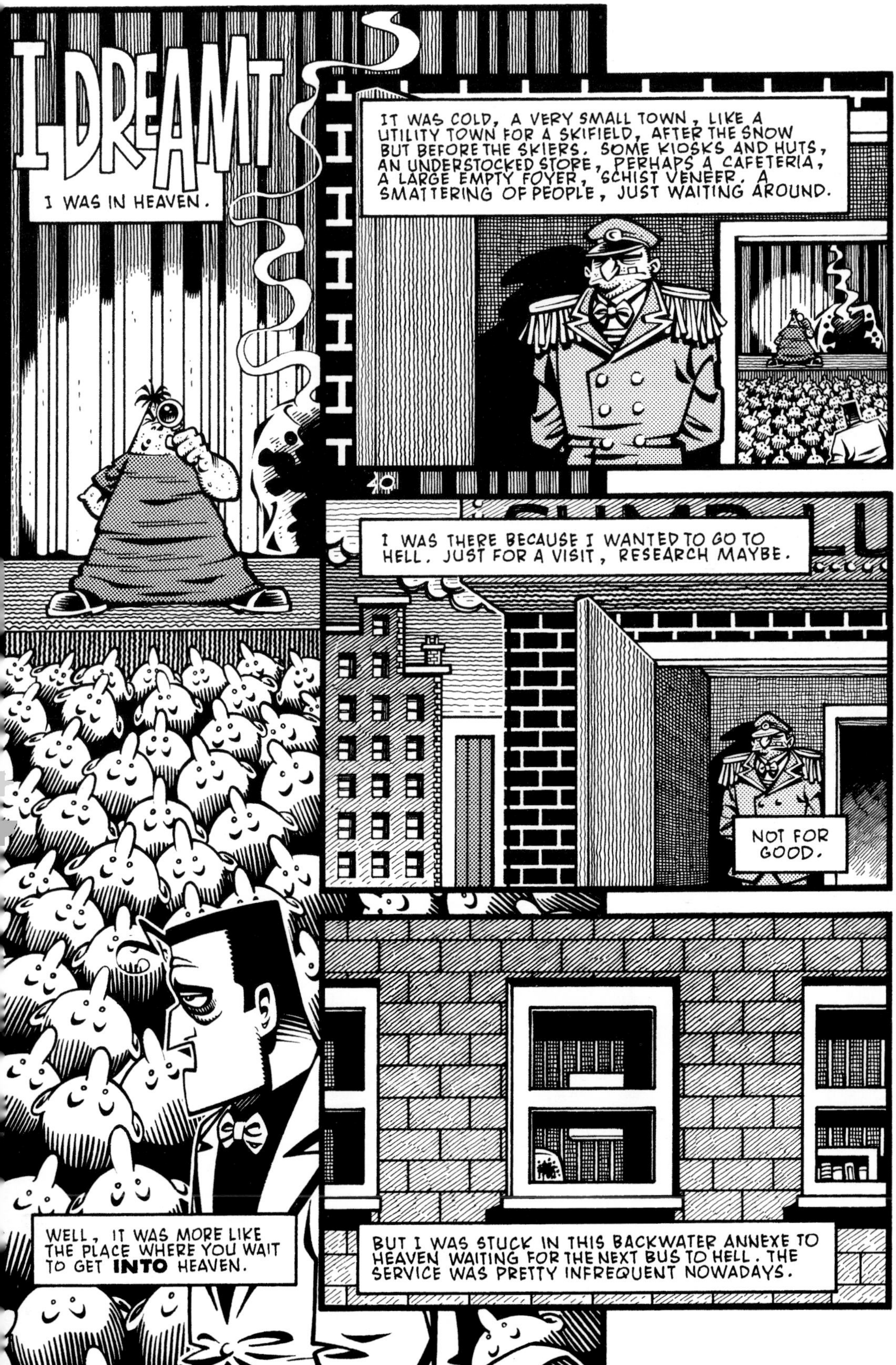
I DREAMT
I WAS IN HEAVEN.
IT WAS COLD, A VERY SMALL TOWN, LIKE A UTILITY TOWN FOR A SKIFIELD, AFTER THE SNOW BUT BEFORE THE SKIERS. SOME KIOSKS AND HUTS, AN UNDERSTOCKED STORE, PERHAPS A CAFETERIA, A LARGE EMPTY FOYER, SCHIST VENEER, A SMATTERING OF PEOPLE, JUST WAITING AROUND.
I WAS THERE BECAUSE I WANTED TO GO TO HELL. JUST FOR A VISIT, RESEARCH MAYBE.
NOT FOR GOOD.
WELL, IT WAS MORE LIKE THE PLACE WHERE YOU WAIT TO GET **INTO** HEAVEN.
BUT I WAS STUCK IN THIS BACKWATER ANNEXE TO HEAVEN WAITING FOR THE NEXT BUS TO HELL. THE SERVICE WAS PRETTY INFREQUENT NOWADAYS.

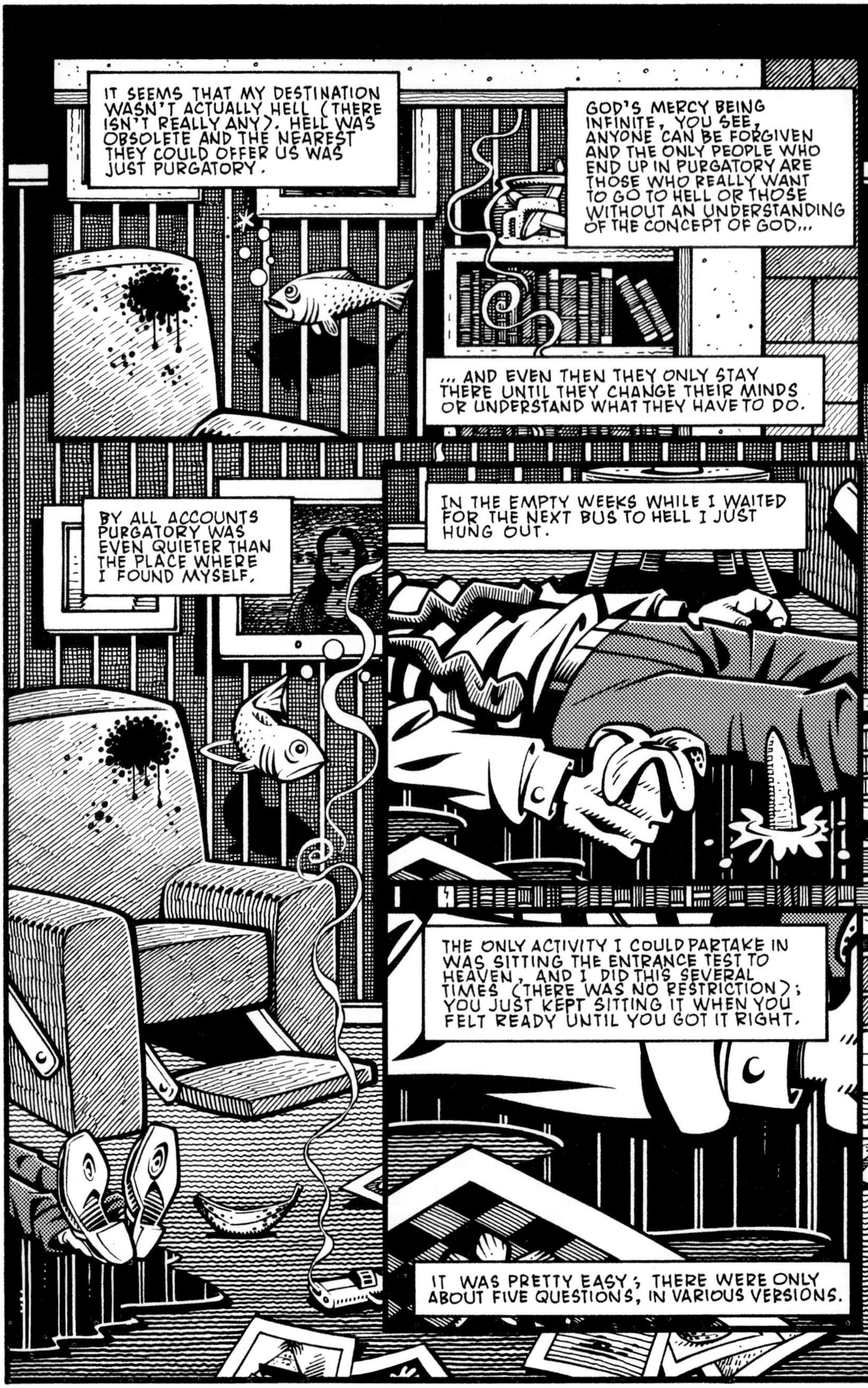
IT SEEMS THAT MY DESTINATION WASN'T ACTUALLY HELL (THERE ISN'T REALLY ANY). HELL WAS OBSOLETE AND THE NEAREST THEY COULD OFFER US WAS JUST PURGATORY.
GOD'S MERCY BEING INFINITE, YOU SEE, ANYONE CAN BE FORGIVEN AND THE ONLY PEOPLE WHO END UP IN PURGATORY ARE THOSE WHO REALLY WANT TO GO TO HELL OR THOSE WITHOUT AN UNDERSTANDING OF THE CONCEPT OF GOD...
... AND EVEN THEN THEY ONLY STAY THERE UNTIL THEY CHANGE THEIR MINDS OR UNDERSTAND WHAT THEY HAVE TO DO.
BY ALL ACCOUNTS PURGATORY WAS EVEN QUIETER THAN THE PLACE WHERE I FOUND MYSELF.
IN THE EMPTY WEEKS WHILE I WAITED FOR THE NEXT BUS TO HELL I JUST HUNG OUT.
THE ONLY ACTIVITY I COULD PARTAKE IN WAS SITTING THE ENTRANCE TEST TO HEAVEN, AND I DID THIS SEVERAL TIMES (THERE WAS NO RESTRICTION); YOU JUST KEPT SITTING IT WHEN YOU FELT READY UNTIL YOU GOT IT RIGHT.
IT WAS PRETTY EASY; THERE WERE ONLY ABOUT FIVE QUESTIONS, IN VARIOUS VERSIONS.

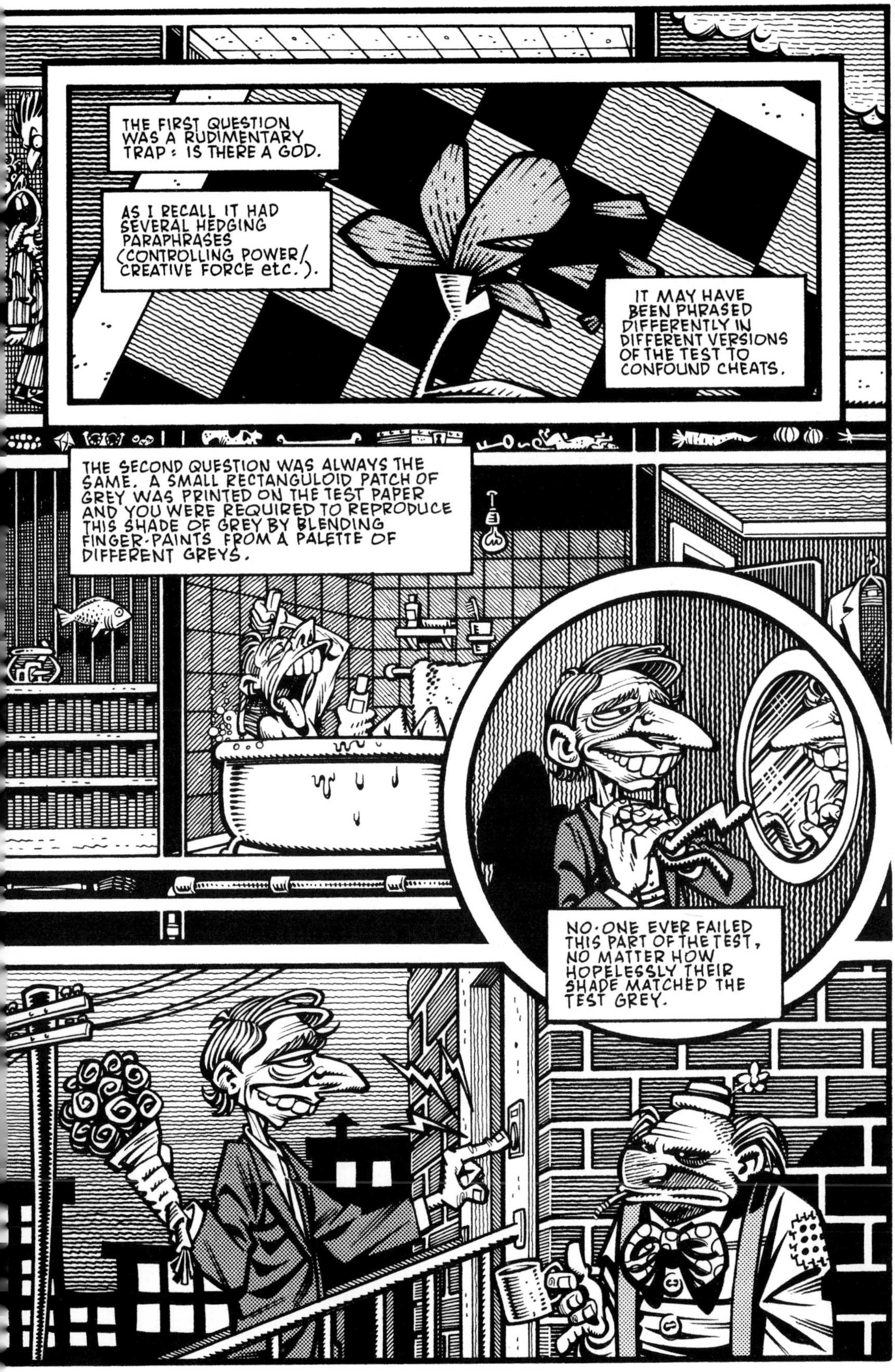
THE FIRST QUESTION WAS A RUDIMENTARY TRAP : IS THERE A GOD.
AS I RECALL IT HAD SEVERAL HEDGING PARAPHRASES (CONTROLLING POWER/ CREATIVE FORCE etc.).
IT MAY HAVE BEEN PHRASED DIFFERENTLY IN DIFFERENT VERSIONS OF THE TEST TO CONFOUND CHEATS.
THE SECOND QUESTION WAS ALWAYS THE SAME. A SMALL RECTANGULOID PATCH OF GREY WAS PRINTED ON THE TEST PAPER AND YOU WERE REQUIRED TO REPRODUCE THIS SHADE OF GREY BY BLENDING FINGER-PAINTS FROM A PALETTE OF DIFFERENT GREYS.
NO-ONE EVER FAILED THIS PART OF THE TEST, NO MATTER HOW HOPELESSLY THEIR SHADE MATCHED THE TEST GREY.

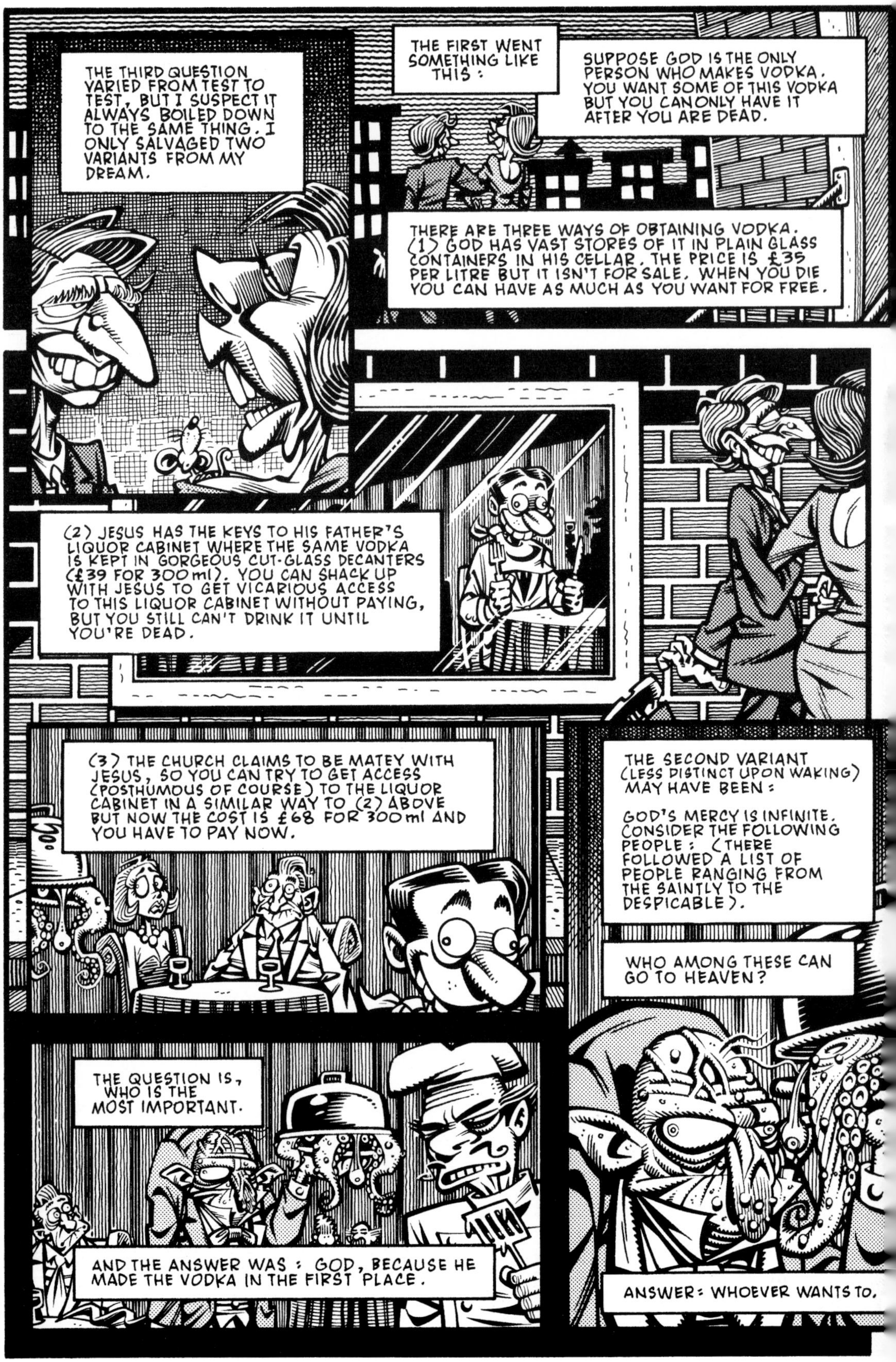
THE THIRD QUESTION VARIED FROM TEST TO TEST, BUT I SUSPECT IT ALWAYS BOILED DOWN TO THE SAME THING. I ONLY SALVAGED TWO VARIANTS FROM MY DREAM.
THE FIRST WENT SOMETHING LIKE THIS:
SUPPOSE GOD IS THE ONLY PERSON WHO MAKES VODKA. YOU WANT SOME OF THIS VODKA BUT YOU CAN ONLY HAVE IT AFTER YOU ARE DEAD.
THERE ARE THREE WAYS OF OBTAINING VODKA. (1) GOD HAS VAST STORES OF IT IN PLAIN GLASS CONTAINERS IN HIS CELLAR. THE PRICE IS £35 PER LITRE BUT IT ISN'T FOR SALE. WHEN YOU DIE YOU CAN HAVE AS MUCH AS YOU WANT FOR FREE.
(2) JESUS HAS THE KEYS TO HIS FATHER'S LIQUOR CABINET WHERE THE SAME VODKA IS KEPT IN GORGEOUS CUT-GLASS DECANTERS (£39 FOR 300ml). YOU CAN SHACK UP WITH JESUS TO GET VICARIOUS ACCESS TO THIS LIQUOR CABINET WITHOUT PAYING, BUT YOU STILL CAN'T DRINK IT UNTIL YOU'RE DEAD.
(3) THE CHURCH CLAIMS TO BE MATEY WITH JESUS, SO YOU CAN TRY TO GET ACCESS (POSTHUMOUS OF COURSE) TO THE LIQUOR CABINET IN A SIMILAR WAY TO (2) ABOVE BUT NOW THE COST IS £68 FOR 300ml AND YOU HAVE TO PAY NOW.
THE QUESTION IS, WHO IS THE MOST IMPORTANT.
AND THE ANSWER WAS: GOD, BECAUSE HE MADE THE VODKA IN THE FIRST PLACE.
THE SECOND VARIANT (LESS DISTINCT UPON WAKING) MAY HAVE BEEN:
GOD'S MERCY IS INFINITE. CONSIDER THE FOLLOWING PEOPLE: (THERE FOLLOWED A LIST OF PEOPLE RANGING FROM THE SAINTLY TO THE DESPICABLE).
WHO AMONG THESE CAN GO TO HEAVEN?
ANSWER: WHOEVER WANTS TO.

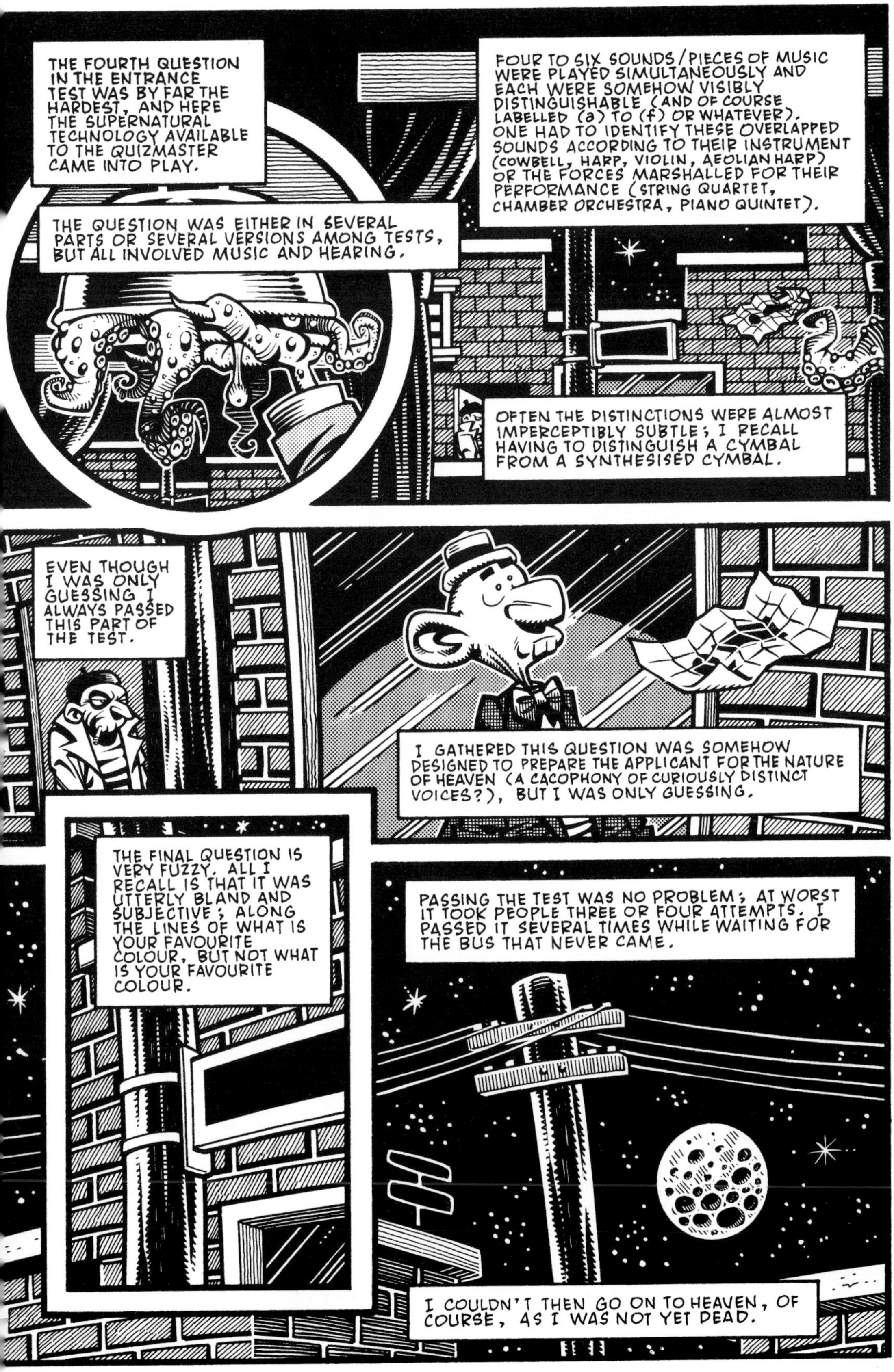
THE FOURTH QUESTION IN THE ENTRANCE TEST WAS BY FAR THE HARDEST, AND HERE THE SUPERNATURAL TECHNOLOGY AVAILABLE TO THE QUIZMASTER CAME INTO PLAY.
THE QUESTION WAS EITHER IN SEVERAL PARTS OR SEVERAL VERSIONS AMONG TESTS, BUT ALL INVOLVED MUSIC AND HEARING.
FOUR TO SIX SOUNDS/PIECES OF MUSIC WERE PLAYED SIMULTANEOUSLY AND EACH WERE SOMEHOW VISIBLY DISTINGUISHABLE (AND OF COURSE LABELLED (a) TO (f) OR WHATEVER). ONE HAD TO IDENTIFY THESE OVERLAPPED SOUNDS ACCORDING TO THEIR INSTRUMENT (COWBELL, HARP, VIOLIN, AEOLIAN HARP) OR THE FORCES MARSHALLED FOR THEIR PERFORMANCE (STRING QUARTET, CHAMBER ORCHESTRA, PIANO QUINTET).
OFTEN THE DISTINCTIONS WERE ALMOST IMPERCEPTIBLY SUBTLE; I RECALL HAVING TO DISTINGUISH A CYMBAL FROM A SYNTHESISED CYMBAL.
EVEN THOUGH I WAS ONLY GUESSING I ALWAYS PASSED THIS PART OF THE TEST.
I GATHERED THIS QUESTION WAS SOMEHOW DESIGNED TO PREPARE THE APPLICANT FOR THE NATURE OF HEAVEN (A CACOPHONY OF CURIOUSLY DISTINCT VOICES?), BUT I WAS ONLY GUESSING.
THE FINAL QUESTION IS VERY FUZZY. ALL I RECALL IS THAT IT WAS UTTERLY BLAND AND SUBJECTIVE; ALONG THE LINES OF WHAT IS YOUR FAVOURITE COLOUR, BUT NOT WHAT IS YOUR FAVOURITE COLOUR.
PASSING THE TEST WAS NO PROBLEM; AT WORST IT TOOK PEOPLE THREE OR FOUR ATTEMPTS. I PASSED IT SEVERAL TIMES WHILE WAITING FOR THE BUS THAT NEVER CAME.
I COULDN'T THEN GO ON TO HEAVEN, OF COURSE, AS I WAS NOT YET DEAD.

BLARDY BLARDY BLARDY BLARDY
BLARDY BLARDY BLARDY
BLARDY BLARDY BLARDY BLARDY
BLARDY BLARDY BLARDY
BLARDY BLARDY BLARDY BLARDY
BLARDY BLARDY BLARDY
BLARDY BLARDY BLARDY BLARDY
BLARDY BLARDY BLARDY
BLARDY BLARDY BLARDY BLARDY
BLARDY BLARDY BLARDY
BLARDY BLARDY BLARDY BLARDY
BLARDY BLARDY BLARDY
BLARDY BLARDY BLARDY BLARDY
BLARDY BLARDY BLARDY
BLARDY BLARDY BLARDY BLARDY
BLARDY BLARDY BLARDY